21 HACKS to ROCK *your* MIDLIFE

RELEASE THE PAST, DARE TO DREAM AND CREATE YOUR LEGACY!

CAT COLUCCIO

First published 2021 by Cat Coluccio

Produced by Indie Experts P/L, Australasia
indieexperts.com.au

Copyright © Cat Coluccio 2021

The moral right of the author to be identified as the author of this work has been asserted.

All rights reserved. Except as permitted under the *Australian Copyright Act 1968*, no part of this publication may be reproduced, stored in a retrieval system, or transmitted in any form or by any means, electronic, mechanical, photocopying, recording or otherwise, without prior written permission from the publisher. All enquiries should be made to the author.

Cover design by Maria Biaggini @ Indie Experts
Internal design by Indie Experts
Typeset in 11.5/15.5 pt Minion Pro by Post Pre-press Group, Brisbane

ISBN 978-0-6487029-7-9 (paperback)
ISBN 978-0-6487029-8-6 (epub)

Disclaimer:

The material in this book is provided for information purposes only. The experiences discussed in this book may not necessarily be the same as the reader's experience. The reader should consult with his or her personal legal, financial and other advisors before utilising the information contained in this book. The author and the publisher assume no responsibility for any damages or losses incurred during or as a result of following this information.

*This book is dedicated to the thousands of
women from around the world who have been
sharing their midlife journeys with me for years
via the Rocking Midlife® Facebook Group.*

*You've made me laugh, you've made me cry. You've challenged
me to think beyond myself and my own culture and most
of all, you've given me a purpose – to serve and encourage
women with the fact that even though life can suck at times –
you can still choose to ROCK your midlife season and beyond!*

CONTENTS

Foreword	vii
Introduction	ix

SECTION 1: AWAKENING — 1
   Hack #1 Be Real — 3
   Hack #2 Accept the Time is Now — 8
   Hack #3 Audit your Life — 15

SECTION 2: RELEASING — 23
   Hack #4 Let go of the Baggage — 25
   Hack #5 Honour the Past But Embrace the Future — 31
   Hack #6 Filter the Voices — 37

SECTION 3: CREATE SPACE — 43
   Hack #7 Declutter your Life – Physical Clutter — 45
   Hack #8 Declutter your Life – Digital Clutter — 52
   Hack #9 Declutter your Life – Mental Clutter — 59

SECTION 4: PROJECT YOU — 71
- Hack #10 What Do You Want? — 73
- Hack #11 What don't you want? — 79
- Hack #12 Research — 84
- Hack #13 Who Will You Need? — 92

SECTION 5: READY TO LAUNCH — 97
- Hack #14 Plan — 99
- Hack #15 Setting up for Success — 108
- Hack #16 Get the Family Buy-In — 117

SECTION 6: LIFT OFF! — 123
- Hack #17 Ditch the Perfectionism! — 125
- Hack #18 Take Action Every Single Day! — 131
- Hack #19 Act Regardless — 139

SECTION 7: LEGACY — 145
- Hack #20 Design your Legacy — 147
- Hack #21 Own your Own Spotlight! — 152

A Final Word From Cat — 159
About Cat Coluccio — 161
Want More Cat? — 163
Acknowledgements — 165

FOREWORD

Midlife isn't an age. It's an experience, one that's far richer and more rewarding with a personal guide to light the way. In Cat's latest book, you have that experienced guide – a powerful, insightful Midlife Master, to lead the way to a more enriching Midlife & Beyond experience than ever before.

Through Cat's personal story, her wisdom and her ingenious "Life Hacks," she provides you with a brilliant roadmap, one written through the eyes of a Midlife woman with decades of life experience under her belt.

Cat's latest book provides women at Midlife & Beyond with all the tools they need to envision, create and rock their best life. Through her years of coaching Midlife women, Cat has a unique perspective and vantage point to be a trusted, authentic voice and leader for the 40 plus woman in the process of reinvention.

This book is meant to be savored, experienced and enjoyed. It's also here to propel you to an entirely new second, third or fourth act! It is loaded with valuable exercises to allow you to let go of the past and to make way for a future filled with purpose, passion and possibility. Cat believes that anything is possible as long as you believe in yourself.

I believe in Cat and I believe in you. Now, go rock that Midlife!

Catherine Grace O'Connell
Chief Executive Cat-Alyst Forever Fierce Media
May 2021

INTRODUCTION

Have you ever looked at yourself in the mirror?
I mean, *really* looked at yourself?
And discovered – with some shock – that there are wrinkles, grey tufts of hair, as well as – *heaven forbid* – chin hairs?
When did they appear?
It feels like we spend our 20s, 30s and much of our 40s rushing around. Juggling the mother-load of child rearing, career advancing, relationship preserving and the multitude of activities associated with each of those things.
Then one day, we stop long enough to look in the mirror.
And it hits us.
We are no longer young women. Our faces and our bodies look and feel different.
The children who we invested so much of ourselves and our identities into, are grown and no longer need us in the same way.

The partner of our younger years has morphed into a middle aged person who we suddenly realise we don't really know, following all of those years of focusing on the kids.

Our parents and elderly relatives are disappearing from our worlds, and the career that we've diligently pursued for what seems like forever, no longer feels fulfilling.

We look into the eyes of that person in the mirror – albeit with slightly fuzzy vision as we've forgotten where we left our reading glasses …

And we think to ourselves.

Is this it?

*Is this **really** it?*

Is this all my life was meant to be?

Maybe you are in this place right now.
Maybe you've been stuck in this place for some time.
Maybe you've actually given up on yourself completely after putting your heart and soul into raising your children.
Maybe you've shelved all of those dreams you once had because now, *you are too old.*

You've missed the boat.

The younger generation are so much smarter, computer-savvy and courageous than you.

INTRODUCTION

You have nothing to offer.

Well honey, I'm here to tell you that **nothing could be further from the truth!**

Your midlife years bring with them so much possibility ...

The possibility of self discovery.

The possibility of adventure.

The possibility of reinvention – and so much more – **IF you choose to pursue them!**

In my decade of working with women in their 40s and beyond, I've noticed that women tend to fall into a number of camps when they hit their midlife years:

The first group are determined to fight the ageing creep all the way, doing their utmost to appear young, hip and competitive with the up-and-coming millennials who are taking over their workplaces.

These women are the first to try any new beauty products and procedures. They are religious about their organic diets and stringent workouts, and they pride themselves on how efficient and committed they are at work, often seen striding purposefully towards the board room, whilst swigging from a protein shaker. *I call these women the Kims.*

The second group are the polar opposite. They were the earth mothers who sat on every PTA board and whose children never tasted sugar or soft drink until they left for college, resulting in said progeny being discovered in sugar comas at the back of lecture rooms, clutching empty energy drink cans to their chests.

These ladies poured every bit of themselves and more into child raising and by default – husband raising. There was only one boss of this household, and there was no contest as mother always knew best. *These Sharons find themselves lost and bewildered at midlife when the centre of their universe leaves home without a backward glance, and their long-suffering extra child / husband is now a simmering pot of resentment.*

Then we come to group three. Ladies who decide to embrace midlife and then some. Think of these ladies like the popular cool girls of our teen years who were gorgeous and knew it.

Sporting long, luxurious silver-grey locks, these ladies are genetic freaks with their modelesque long slim limbs and high cheekbones. Often seen wearing designer activewear and pictured in complicated yoga poses in front of the setting sun on perfect beaches, *these Deborahs are the curators of aspirational blogs and Instagram accounts.* Every midlife woman wants to look like them and live their lifestyle – just like every teen girl wanted to look like Cindy Crawford or Elle MacPhearson back in the day.

And then there is the average, ordinary, every day midlife woman just like you and me. We are the ones who've noticed the addition of some midlife comfort kilos. We dabble with healthy eating and plant-based food trends whilst keeping a firm grip on our glass of Prosecco or vodka and tonic, with our other hand reaching for the crackers and cheese.

We check out Botox and facial lasering when the sales are on, otherwise we are a dab hand with the most beloved and essential beauty tool of midlife women everywhere – the tweezers.

We love our children, rub along okay with our partners or are well used to single life and adore our fur-babies, yet deep down, we aren't satisfied.

Deep down, there is a niggle, a stirring that just won't go away.

There's a quiet little voice whispering inside every morning when the alarm wakes us up:

Is this it?

When we stop and look at ourselves in the mirror, we ask ourselves that same question out loud:

Is this it?

You're reading this book for a reason, and I can guarantee that is because deep inside, you know that midlife is NOT it!

Your best years are NOT behind you!

You were made for more.

You have **so** much more to do, and more importantly, to ***become!***

And reading these 21 Hacks is going to help you kick into gear and start moving from stuck towards living that purposeful life you desire!

Grab yourself a pen and notebook and buckle in as we peel back the layers of WHO you are, before getting clear on who you WANT to be, what you WANT to do and HOW you are going to get there!

In short, we are on a mission together to help you ROCK your midlife years and beyond with purpose and passion.

Let's do this!

Cat x

PS: Want a FREE e-book to inspire you to make the most of your midlife season? Get *5 Tips to Make your Midlife ROCK* here: www.rockmidlife.com

SECTION 1

AWAKENING

"If every day is an awakening, you will never grow old. You will just keep growing."

~ GAIL SHEEHY

HACK #1
Be Real

> "It's bad timing, but a lot of kids become teenagers just as their parents are hitting their mid-life crisis. So everybody's miserable and confused and seeking that new sense of identity."
> ~ LAURIE HALSE ANDERSON

I've heard it said by many people that a little piece of you disappears when you get married. It makes sense when you consider that you are knitting your life together with someone else. There's got to be some compromise, some rubbing off of the hard edges as the two become one – otherwise you are in for one bumpy ride!

The exchange of "me" for "we" is something that most of us theoretically understand what we are entering into when we sign on the dotted line of the marriage license. However, the true outworking of this union of two individuals is not really felt until years later, when the organic meshing of two lives has well and truly taken place.

Talk to any widow, any divorcee or indeed *any* woman who has emerged from a long term relationship – regardless of if it was a happy union or otherwise. Not only is there the shock of whatever situation brought about their single status, but also the common feeling of "*I don't know who I am without them.*"

Interestingly, there are many happily married women at midlife also saying this very same thing, and I know this firsthand, as I was one of them. It's as if the numbing balm of busy family life wears off at midlife and you end up faced with the reality that along with the perky breasts and wrinkle free face of your youth, you have lost the sense of who YOU really are.

Beyond the physical change however, lies a bigger question – *the one of whether the dreams you held dear as a young woman are still there.* Those dreams might be buried deep under years of serving your family and others, but the reality is, the young woman with her many hopes and aspirations who you once were, is still part of you.

The question now though? Are these dreams that you want to dig up, dust off and reconsider, or is it time to let go of the "what ifs" and start dreaming a new dream altogether? Be warned though, as this period of considering which path to take can bring up all sorts of emotions, and whilst you might not think that you blame your partner or even yourself, you might get a shock at what feelings rise to the surface when reality starts to bite:

When did I choose to let go of the part of me that wanted to pursue a certain career path?

When did I decide to walk away from the dreams I held of writing books, or creating art, or running my own business or launching my non-profit?

When did I settle?

Why did I settle?

Some women choose to blame their partner and fracture their marriage as they desperately try to regain their youthful years. Other women however, realise that although there may be very real issues to be addressed with their partner – the real culprit behind your leaving those dreams and plans behind – *is you.*

Now bear with me here. I'd prefer that you don't shoot the messenger, but I'm going to get real with you by saying something that will possibly push your buttons …

Honey, it's time that you acknowledged that **you** *are the one who abdicated your role of pursuing those hopes and dreams.*

Yes, I know that life can be harsh and someone reading this may have been the victim of horrendous partnerships and life circumstances that were completely out of their control and crushed their spirit. If that is you, I am so sorry and hope that you have received the professional support that you need to heal. I also believe however, that if you *are* reading this book, it's because you harbour a deep desire to take back your power and create the purposeful life and career that *you* want – and I'm here to encourage you to do just that.

The reality is, there are countless stories in history of people who endured the bleakest of situations – and the ones that were the most resilient, the ones that went on to rebuild better lives – were the ones who realised that ultimately, ***they*** held the key to their hopes and dreams – not someone else.

And midlife is when we pause long enough to consider this very thing, which leads to three questions:
- Have I become the kind of person that I aspired to be?
- Am I living the life that I aspired to?
- Am I doing the work that I felt I was called to do?

Before you go forward, you need to look back in order to reflect and learn, so grab that paper and pen and launch into your first Action Task.

ACTION TASKS:

- Find a quiet place where you won't be interrupted. Make sure that you have your paper and pen handy, a glass of water and some tissues as chances are, you will get emotional at some point – *and that's okay!*

- Think about, and then write the answers to these questions:
  1. Am I the person now that I aspired to be as a teen?
  2. What are my favourable traits?
     E.g. I am a generous person.
  3. What are my not so favourable traits?
     E.g: I get resentful easily.
  4. Is there a time in my life when I let myself down?
  5. Is there a time in my life when I was hurt by someone else's words and didn't pursue my goal as a result?

- Once you have answered these questions, writing as much detail as you can, I want to you get up, jog on the spot, do some star jumps and get the blood pumping. Let's change your state physically as that will also help you emotionally. You are being completely honest with yourself in this first hack and whilst it will in all probability sting emotionally at times, the idea is to not make you so distraught that you can't move ahead into the next few hacks which will help you reframe and move forward.

HACK #2
Accept the Time is Now

> "Midlife: when the Universe grabs your shoulders and tells you 'I'm not f-ing around, use the gifts you were given'."
>
> ~ DR. BRENÉ BROWN

This quote from Brené Brown has become the rallying cry for midlife women worldwide who are looking down the barrel of their midlife years and wondering *who the hell am I and what the hell do I do now?*

Think of midlife as being a huge crossroad with a sign pointing in all directions. It's not a crossroad that you arrive at precisely the day you turn 40 or 50 – rather, it is a crossroad that sneaks up on you while you are busy with other things. It's exactly the same as when you drive a familiar route every day, so much so that your inner auto-pilot switches on, and you find yourself at your destination, wondering how on earth you got there.

I don't know about you, but my memories of my 20s and 30s are a bit of a blur as I was so busy juggling children, school runs, meals, laundry and trying to snatch moments with my husband between sports events, my own work and laundry. *Yes I mentioned laundry twice. The washing machine and I had a very intimate relationship – it would be fascinating to read a study on how much of our life is spent doing laundry – especially when you have sporty children who train most days and a husband who loves fishing!*

And then one day, it hit me – I was about to become redundant and I had some choices to make. I wrote about this realisation in my first book *Girl, Get over yourself and get in the Game!* It didn't happen the day I turned 40 though, instead, the day I found myself at the great midlife crossroads, was the day that my youngest child was accepted into university when I was 43. For the previous 6 years, I had put everything aside to homeschool my two teens who were both at elite levels with their sports. Homeschooling enabled them to literally travel the world competing, while still getting an education and having time for friends and hobbies such as RC racing, crafts and music.

I loved those years, and my husband and I did all we could to shuttle our son and our daughter around the city to their various training sessions which each averaged around 17–20 hours a week. Weekends were full of games, events and championships.

I had become super mum. I was a taxi-driving, snack-preparing, education-supervising ninja with particular skills in teen negotiation and persuasion – and of course, *highly* developed laundry skills.

And I loved it.

I kept my blinkers firmly on when the first signs signalling the end of this season started, as my older child entered a tertiary training school, then headed off to Germany for a period of time to play soccer. I still had 2 years of homeschooling left with my daughter and chose to ignore the ticking clock of change. My 40th birthday came and went, and whilst there was the occasional niggle of unrest, I firmly squashed it down and continued my busy life of being super ninja mum extraordinaire. I even started a small photography business on the side. When my daughter was playing gigs in her band, I was the roadie and photographer in the background. Full circle given the many years she watched her mother performing on stage.

Then those packages in the mail arrived, announcing that she had been offered multiple places at two universities and whilst I was thrilled for her, my stomach was churning. I had walked smack into that signpost at the midlife crossroad and my life was about to be changed forever. *How the heck did I get here?*

The universe wasn't grabbing me by the shoulders, it was slapping me firmly across both cheeks and I had a decision to make. In the game show of life, I had 3 options. I could pine for what I had – those wonderful years of watching my children thrive and develop – or I could try to find my way back to what I once knew – teaching high schoolers, lecturing and taking on private music students.

Or – *I could reinvent myself completely and create a new future.*

I chose box number 3 – the new future – and launched into the unknown to go back to school alongside students younger than my own kids, in order to become a personal trainer. I was an overweight, completely unfit home-schooling mother in her 40s, but thankfully the training school accepted me and that initial decision was the first step that led to over a decade of evolving experiences and achievements that I could never have foreseen back that day when I sat alongside my excited daughter and her pile of offers on our back deck.

I tell this story often to women who are waiting for the clouds to part, the angelic chorus to sing and the parchment to descend from heaven, inscribed with these words: "Welcome to midlife. You will now do this___, live here___, earn this___, then retire as a happy, financially secure, partnered grandmother with your cherubic grandchildren dancing at your knees."

Sorry to break it to you, but life doesn't quite work like that!

There is no "official" start to midlife, but if you can pause long enough from the busyness of your life, you will start to hear your own little voice, deep inside asking *"is this it?"*

Is this all there is to my life?

That's your indication that the crossroads are near, and you can continue on blindly until you slam into the signpost like me, or start tuning in to that inner voice now. Once you do, it will be time to change the question from *is this it?* to *what if?*

ACTION TASKS:

- Grab your trusty notebook, a stack of coloured pencils and a timer.
- Draw a big circle in the middle of a page, labelled "Me" then set the timer for 20 minutes. The entire exercise is to be done in this timeframe as taking any longer means that you will start to reason and overthink. The idea with this exercise is to dream and explore.
- Down the left side of the paper, draw lots of smaller circles and in them, write down all of the hats that you currently wear. Some examples might be "mother," "wife," "dental receptionist," "teacher," "real estate agent."
- Underneath the "ME" in the middle circle, write the words *what if?*
- Down the right-hand side, draw more small circles and in them, list all of the things that you would *want* to be if time and money were no issue. Some hats might still be the same, e.g. "mother," "wife," but there might be others there too like "author," "painter," "fitness instructor,"
- Using your coloured pencils, colour any of the bubbles that appear on both sides of the paper. You'll be able to get a bird's eye view of what parts of your current life you want to take forward into your next season.

The idea is not to restrict your *"what if?"* in any way whatsoever. This is all about pushing any perfectionist or negative thinking aside and simply allowing yourself to imagine. There may be 5 totally different, unrelated careers or pursuits on your list but that's okay. It's important to allow yourself to dream of all the possibilities before narrowing it down to where you will start.

That part is coming, but not today.
Today you dream.

HACK #3
Audit your Life

> "Life can only be understood backwards; but it must be lived forwards."
> ~ SØREN KIERKEGAARD

There is a particular exercise that I do with every client that I work with, and that is the Wheel of Life exercise, made popular by the late, great Zig Ziglar. It is a fabulous way of taking a snapshot of where your life is at in this very moment, and I not only included it as one of the hacks in my original 21 Hacks book, *21 Hacks to ROCK your Life!*, I also wrote a workbook with an accompanying video called *Your Life Audit* to help walk people through the process.

Undertaking a Life Audit will bring up a mixed bag of emotions. You will be taking a snapshot of where your life is right now, and I can guarantee that not only will you have some areas of your life that you are progressing in and feel great about – you'll also have some areas that you have been ignoring for some time as they suck, so it's easier to keep the blinkers on rather than deal with them.

Think of those times when you look under the bed and are shocked to discover the pile of rubbish that has accumulated. Logically, you knew it was there, but you ignored it – "out of sight, out of mind" *right?* The reality of just how large that pile has grown can be a real surprise. That surprise is what you are probably going to experience when you undertake your Life Audit. You will feel like a failure in some areas of your life, will hopefully feel like you have your act together in other areas, and you will possibly be shocked at the crap that has accumulated in yet other areas – all whilst you were steadfastly looking the other way during the past few years.

Let me give you some examples. The Wheel of Life exercise can be personalised in lots of ways, however I generally stick to the most common 8 areas of life when working with clients. These areas are:
- Romance
- Recreation
- Career
- Personal Development
- Finances
- Health
- Environment
- Relationships

The idea is to give all of these areas a rating out of 10, 1 being the lowest, 10 being the highest. You can then see very clearly exactly which areas of your life are doing well at the moment, and which areas aren't.

Remember those fun school reports you used to bring home to your parents with great trepidation each year? Think of your Life Audit like that – but without the trepidation as there is no judgement here! You are playing all 3 characters in this process – that of the teacher conducting the exercise, that of the pupil who has to answer honestly, and that of the parent who assesses the results and makes decisions accordingly.

Taking the time to audit your life is one of the best exercises you can undertake at midlife. The snapshot of your life as it is right now gives you the information you need to assess and make decisions on in order to support you as you head into your next season.

For instance ...

Are you happy with the physical environment of your home and workplace? Is it conducive to productivity? Does it make you feel calm and secure or does it distract you with clutter in every room? Do the voices of your co-workers echoing through the office get on your nerves?

Are you happy to live with your physical environment going forward, or is this an area that you want to transform in your next season?

How about another one? How is your love-life going at the moment? Are you in a committed relationship that is fulfilling, or are you looking to be in one? Have you found that there are things missing? Do you look at your partner some mornings and think "who on earth are you?" Do you want more spark, more joy, more shared times of intimacy? Have you been settling for much less than what you know you are worth?

What are you going to do about it in your next season?

Then there is your career. Are you in a job that you love that gives you purpose and respect, or do you resent leaving the house every morning to go and work there? Are you fulfilled, on fire and enjoying your workplace, or do you harbour a secret desire to leave the job world and become your own boss?

How are you going to change things up in your next season?

These are questions that you possibly won't have the answers for right away – *and that is to be expected.* It's one thing to take a snapshot of your life in one sitting, getting a broad idea of which areas you are happy with and which areas you totally want to change – and another altogether to thoroughly analyse your results and create a transformative action plan.

The results of this exercise have the potential to be overwhelming if you've never undertaken a Life Audit before, which is why it is so important to leave your inner judge at the door.

You are *not* silly for staying in the job that you are not passionate about, but is paying your bills. You are *not* a failure for having a cluttered home, and you have *not* left it too late to take action on improving your marriage, your health or your dreams.

Here's a secret – *no-one has their life all together!* Regardless of what their amazingly perfect Instagram content might suggest, you are not to compare your life in this moment to someone else's perfectly curated highlight reel. Of course you already know this logically, but I need you to know this in your heart, so that you can go ahead and undertake the Wheel of Life exercise being completely honest with your answers, without being harsh and judgemental of yourself.

ACTION STEPS:

Below are the very steps that I outline in *21 Hacks to ROCK your Life!* and also in the *Your Life Audit* workbook. Grab a glass of wine or a mug of your favourite warm drink, find somewhere quiet, and get to it!

- Fill out your own Wheel of Life. Get creative and use different colors for each segment as you rate them. Here are the categories along with some prompting questions that you can ask yourself:

    Environment: where you live and where you work. Are you in the midst of the city with all of its noise and bustle? In the suburbs? Near the beach or in a rural setting? Is your work environment stimulating, oppressive or neutral? How does your environment make you feel? Is it conducive to you achieving the things that you want to achieve?

    Career: are you working in a field that interests you or do you want to change completely? Are you satisfied with your earnings, your potential for development, your co-workers, your boss?

    Finances: are you earning enough to survive? Are you struggling? Have you got limiting beliefs around money that hold you back? Are you unsure of how to invest your money? Are you wanting to earn more?

Health: how are you feeling energetically? Are you eating/sleeping/hydrating well? Are you moving your body and participating in resistance training? Are you having regular wellness and dental check-ups?

Relationships: do you make time to socialise with your family and friends? Are there relationships that you have let slip and want to repair? Have you been so busy that you feel lonely?

Romance: are you wanting to find a partner but don't have the time? Is your relationship with your partner strong or have you been neglecting it?

Personal Development: are you the same person you were ten years ago or have you grown in outlook, thinking and achievement? Do you make time to read, learn and study? Have you undertaken any new classes, be they academic, physical or artistic, to continue your personal development?

Recreation: do you take time for regular social outings? Do you book regular holidays? Do you allow time for hobbies and fun activities?

- Which areas are you happy with?
- Which areas stand out as not being where you would ideally like them to be?
- What are your initial thoughts about things you would

like to transform in your life as you head into your next season?
- Now put all of the pens and papers aside, crank some loud music and dance around for a few minutes. Leave your Ms Judgy hat at the door and give yourself a huge hug. Go on – do it! You are an amazing lady who has done your best to this point in time, so celebrate yourself!

Section 2

RELEASING

"When I let go of what I am,
I become what I might be."

~ LAO TZU

HACK #4
Let go of the Baggage

> "Take a walk through the garden of forgiveness and pick a flower of forgiveness for everything you have ever done. When you get to that time that is now, make a full and total forgiveness of your entire life and smile at the bouquet in your hands because it truly is beautiful."
> ~ STEPHEN RICHARDS

You don't reach midlife without a few hefty suitcases of baggage.

Those 15 odd times you fell off the diet wagon over the past 20 years? Baggage.

That time you drank one too many wines and tore strips off your partner in front of everyone at a friend's party? Baggage.

The times you yelled at your kids in utter frustration when they caused you to run late for work yet again? Baggage.

The times you stuffed up at work and tried to blame it on a co-worker but got caught out? Baggage?

That divorce you didn't see coming? Baggage.

The loss of your parent to cancer? Baggage.

That season of estrangement from your teenager? Baggage.

Some of the baggage gets left behind as you rush through your busy life, and that's a good thing. Unfortunately though, it's generally not much as you are so practised at holding tight to all of your baggage, and when you stop at that signpost at the crossroads of midlife, you suddenly feel the true weight of everything you have been carrying.

Shame, embarrassment, fear, anger, frustration, self-loathing, sorrow …

Baggage comes in different shapes and forms, yet every type has the same effect – it weighs you down. If not careful, that weight becomes so much that you stop moving forward altogether, and instead start putting down roots tinged with bitterness and disappointment. These are then fertilised by envy when you see others around you living fulfilling and purposeful lives.

One of the byproducts of completing a Life Audit is that you suddenly become acutely aware of your baggage once that Life Wheel drawing revealing all of your low points is laid out in front of you. It is hard to keep your "positive thinking" blinkers on when you can clearly see where your life is not working, and it is in this moment that you have a choice:

You can choose to remain where you are, clutching your heavy baggage and acutely aware of your failings, disappointments and shortcomings …

OR

You can choose to accept that you have made mistakes, lean in to the uncomfortable feelings of grief and disappointment, ask for forgiveness from others where applicable, then forgive yourself and let your baggage go.

The reality is, in order for you to move forward, to transform and to give yourself the gift of ROCKING your midlife season and beyond – you have to face this choice. Avoiding it like you've avoided other hard decisions in the past will still bring a result: the same result laid out in front of you in your Life Wheel.

Can you live another 5/10/20 years in exactly the same place you are in now?

Or do you want better?

It's one thing to leave your past behind, but another entirely to acknowledge it, to take the learnings, to feel the emotions, then to close the chapter by forgiving yourself as well as others who have hurt you or who have wronged you along the way.

Are you ready to forgive yourself so that you can transform your life going forward?

ACTION STEPS:

- Go back to your Life Wheel diagram and questions from HACK #3. What were the areas in your life that you weren't happy with?
- List these on a separate piece of paper, along with any other areas of your life you are disappointed with.
- Next to this list, write who you are hurt and angry with. Your name will probably be the main one listed, but there will be others too so list them, and push aside any false guilt that arises because you are writing their names down. As someone who has had to break free of 2 cultish groups, I know first hand how you can struggle with feeling disloyal even when you know that you are being treated badly.
- Take the time to feel the grief and disappointment reflected in that list. I say this as I don't want to make light of what has happened in your past. There will be very real feelings of sorrow and grief and these need to be acknowledged, so while I will be challenging you to leave these behind, I also know that some wounds are especially deep. This might be the time in your journey where you see a professional therapist to help you work through extremely painful episodes of your life, particularly if they include abuse of any kind.
- Now go through that list of names, and say aloud "I forgive you_____" then consciously let go of the hurt and disappointment of this time / situation. As you do this, cross them off that list.

- Remember the mirror that we talked about at the very beginning of this book? Go and stand in front of it now. Look yourself in the eye and tell your reflection that you forgive yourself for all of the stupid, self-centred and wrong decisions that you have made in the past. Tell your reflection that you accept yourself and that you are committed to doing the work to create the life, and become the person you want to become in your next season.
- Take that list of your faults, your failings and the people who have hurt you, tear it up or throw it in a fire. They are forgiven and you have consciously released them from being your baggage.
- Take the time to pray for God's forgiveness for where you have hurt others in the past, and hand over all of your shame, disappointment and grief.

Now it's time to move forward.

HACK #5
Honour the Past But Embrace the Future

> "Look not mournfully into the past, it comes not back again. Wisely improve the present, it is thine. Go forth to meet the shadowy future without fear and with a manly heart."
>
> ~ HENRY WADSWORTH LONGFELLOW

Remember that year when you and your partner sat together with huge smiles on your faces as you juggled your video camera with one hand while helping your preschoolers open their Christmas presents with the other?

How about that year when your 10 year old son got up and performed in the school play?

Or the other year when your 8 year old daughter shot the winning hoop at the inter-school basketball final?

Then there was your 30th birthday with all of your now deceased older family members and long lost friends in attendance?

These treasured moments in time are the precious memories that you carry with you today. Even the ordinary moments of hanging out washing whilst hearing your kids' laughter as they bounce on the nearby trampoline are precious when those kids have long since grown up and moved on and the trampoline thrown out years ago.

Our lives are shaped by thousands of such moments, and these influence who we are today. When you are at that midlife crossroads however, you have a decision to make regarding these memories, and this decision is not unlike the one you made regarding all of the baggage you have been carrying.

Are you going to keep looking back and pining for what you had – or will you acknowledge and honour your past, while setting your face firmly towards the future and taking the steps necessary in the present to lead you there?

I asked a question about how women deal with the empty nest in my Rocking Midlife® Facebook Group a while ago. Most women responded that they were sad but trying to move on with life. One woman's response really struck me though. She exclaimed that she was devastated. She was crying all the time and wished she could turn back time and go back to when her children were young.

I get that.

Remember my story that I shared at the beginning about having to find a new career due to my homeschooling role being made redundant? That season of time saw my world totally change, and with it, how I defined myself changed too.

I was no longer my children's education facilitator / taxi driver / hands-on mother and it could have been very easy to stay stuck in a place of denial, hanging on to them and to the life we had been living for the previous 6 years.

It would have done them no favours whatsoever though, and it would have been the worst, limiting decision I could make for myself – and honey, the same applies to you right now.

In order for you to create a fabulous, *rocking* midlife adventure, you need to stop hanging on to the past – be it a wonderful past or be it a bitter past. Obviously you keep the memories that count and take the learnings into your future – but it is time for you to consciously put your past behind you where it belongs. Both the pain AND the nostalgia I should add. You need to remember that nostalgia has the potential to warp your perception of history so much that you can end up longing for a fantasy that wasn't really "all that" at the time. If your future is unknown, it can be tempting to lose yourself in this nostalgia in order to delay facing reality.

What's really interesting however, is while we associate nostalgia with "the good old days," the word is actually derived from the Greek word nostos, meaning return to or homecoming, and altos which means to ache or refers to pain. "Nostalgia" therefore really means returning to pain.

> "Never look back. If Cinderella went to pick up her shoe, she would not have become a princess."
>
> ~ ANON.

Are you ready to let go of your past so that you can fully step forward into your future?

ACTION STEPS:

- Grab some of your photos and albums from the time in your life that you particularly miss.
- How do you feel when you see these photos? Try to recall the events and sift through the memories – what are real and what are just nostalgia kicking in?
- Symbolically close those albums and grab your trusty journal and pen, ready to answer the following questions:
    a) *What did you love about the main events that you recall?*
    b) *What did you feel? Who was there? How did these people make you feel?*
- Once you complete these questions, repeat the following words aloud: "I thank you for the memories, and now the chapter is done." There's nothing magical in these words, but the tangible action of writing and speaking will help make the action of releasing the past more real.
- If there was past trauma that really affects you and you struggle to move on, there is no shame in that, but I do recommend that you go see a professional therapist to help work through it so that you can embrace your future.
- Create ONE memory box for any particular letters, moments or cards that you don't want to let go of. One box is the limit though, otherwise you will risk becoming a sentimental hoarder and that brings its own set of issues.

- After doing this fairly intense emotional walk down memory lane, shake yourself off, pump out some loud music and change your mental and emotional state.

It's time to look forward!

HACK #6
Filter the Voices

> "Your inner voice is the voice of divinity. To hear it, we need to be in solitude, even in crowded places."
> ~ A. R. RAHMAN

Do you sometimes feel like you are bombarded with "noise?"

Your email inbox is full to the brim.

Your kitchen countertop holds a messy pile of brochures and catalogues.

You find yourself feeling more and more inadequate whenever you dive down the social media rabbit hole.

Your TV is on constantly as is your radio the second you jump in your car.

Your friends and co-workers are always talking about the state of the world, the economy, their jobs and what they think YOU should be doing.

Your family all have opinions on what they think you should be doing with your life and have no hesitation in sharing them with you.

And these are just the EXTERNAL voices!

On the INSIDE are your own voices telling you over and over that you aren't good enough, you aren't capable enough, you aren't thin enough, pretty enough, clever enough, tall enough, fashionable enough, worthy enough – just NOT enough!

If you are truly wanting to transform or reinvent any area of your life, it's important that you learn to filter the noise, otherwise you risk being buffeted in so many different directions, leading to frustration and disappointment when you don't get to the destination that you *really* want to reach.

Filtering the noise can mean taking practical steps to change some of your habits that are not serving you positively. These habits might be as simple as turning off your radio or TV once you have heard your one 30 minute news update for the day.

It might mean filtering your Facebook feed. Do you really need to be in hundreds of groups? Is it essential that you scroll for hours, commenting on strangers' posts and getting upset when you see how others are seemingly doing better than you?

Who are the people that you allow to speak into your life? Are you listening to people who have different values or who aren't as goal orientated or optimistic as you?

What books are you reading? What music or talkback programs are you listening to? When you remove the negative voices and influences, you need to replace them with something, otherwise the old negative input will slide back in to fill that void.

It's one thing to take a stand for your values amongst your friends and family once or twice. It's an entirely different thing to *always* be in conflict with their ideas and values – especially when it comes to what they think you should be doing.

Filtering the noise – both the external and the internal chatter – enables something special to happen. When you turn down all of those voices, you are able to hear a different voice – that quiet, small voice that is right down deep inside you. This is the voice that whispers that you are made for more. That you are capable of more and that you were born to make a difference. If you don't filter out those other voices however, you will miss this special voice. This soft whisper from your heart will be drowned out by the noise of all of these other voices. When you can't hear it, you risk finding yourself bouncing from idea to idea, constantly second guessing yourself and constantly getting distracted and distressed when you can't settle on a path that feels right for you.

In order to *rock* your midlife, you need to commit to taking action to filter out the noise that is distracting you from pursuing your dreams.

ACTION STEPS:

- Digital detox – scroll through your Facebook page likes and groups, and ask yourself if that page or group supports your vision for your life, or is instead a distraction. Unlike, unfollow and move on – trust me, you won't miss them!

    Likewise, work your way through your packed inbox. Are these emails a distraction or are they adding value to your life? Set yourself a challenge to unsubscribe from as many as possible.

- Now on to your friends and family. Whilst it might feel too harsh to completely wipe someone from your life, think about what boundaries you can put in place to protect your vision and outlook. Instead of having lunch every work day with your workmates who love to gossip about everything negative in the world, restrict yourself to one lunch a week with them, and on the other days, go somewhere quiet where you can be thinking about, writing and planning your new midlife adventure.

    If you have family members or friends who like to phone you every few days for lengthy conversations about people they love to moan about, use a timer or let them know that you are extremely busy at the moment and nominate a certain time once a week to chat. Consciously choose to limit the time spent listening to people who are dream stealers and in the case of family who you do need to spend time with, try your best to steer the conversation away from complaining, to finding out about their dreams and plans. You might be surprised to discover that the aunt who regularly makes you feel silly for wanting more out of life is actually hurting and disappointed with her own lot in life.

- Write yourself a list of "I ams." For every negative voice that you have in your head, reverse what is being said and write that down. For example, your negative voice might be saying you can't build an online business because you've failed in the past. Your reframe might be: "I am capable of building an online business and I'm starting today." Next, add a list of "I ams" that support your reframed statement. For example: "I am not defined by my past," "I am surrounded this time by positive and supportive people," "I am capable of finding the help I need to succeed," "I am working with an amazing coach this time" etc. Aim for at least 20 supporting statements for each reframed negative voice, and reach for these every time that your inner voices get so noisy that they affect your joy and productivity. In time, you will find that the negative inner voice gets softer and softer as the "I ams" drown it out.

SECTION 3

CREATE SPACE

"When you let go, you create space for better things to enter into your life."

~ UNKNOWN

HACK #7

Declutter your Life – Physical Clutter

> "Clutter is not just the stuff on your floor – it's anything that stands between you and the life you want to be living."
>
> ~ PETER WALSH

Hack #4 in my first 21 Hacks book: *21 Hacks to Rock your Life!* talks about how physical clutter can actually be a representation of what is going on in your life. If you find yourself always stressed, feeling like you are unorganised and bouncing from crisis to crisis instead of feeling like you are in the driver's seat of your life – look around youself right now.

What is the state of your desk? Is it covered in bills, stationary and computer cables?

What have you got laying all over your bedroom floor and countertop? Is yesterday's underwear still in the corner? Have you got enough hair products to open your own shop lined up around the basin?

Are your closets full to the brim and about to burst? Have you a pile of handbags and shoes that you swear seems to multiply overnight?

How many of the wardrobes in your house contain items of your clothing? Can you easily find the clothes that you want to wear or are you hard pressed to find anything that isn't the wrong size, stained or uncomfortable?

Then there's the kitchen. Do you feel at ease when you walk through your kitchen and dining room or are the countertops and surfaces full of mail, appliances, charging cables, yesterday's unpacked shopping as well as your car keys and the parcel you were meant to take to the post office?

Clutter is debilitating and depressing. Research has shown that it can lead to reduced productivity as you enter a state of sensory overload when your brain is constantly receiving information via all of your senses, responding to the sight, the sound, the smell and the touch of the clutter all around you. This constant intake of information in turn leads to overwhelm and procrastination – NOT a state that is going to help you to start rocking your midlife season!

I'm a firm believer that the clearing of physical clutter plays a strong part in helping women emotionally let go of the past, while making space for their future. The very act of assessing and deciding on the future of each physical object can be cathartic when you think back to how it came into your life, who it was from, what memories it brings up and if it is time to let it go or instead, bring with you into your next season. There is much merit to Marie Kondo's practice of asking yourself if the object sparks joy – and this question can be applied to the clutter in so many other areas of life too!

There is a concept called "Swedish Death Cleaning," which might sound bleak, yet is actually a very positive and liberating practice. Often coinciding with a desire to downsize, Swedish Death Cleaning refers to the practice of decluttering your home and possessions in order to save the headache of dealing with your clutter being passed on to your family after you die.

Grief brings its own set of challenges, so why add weeks of sorting your clutter to your family who will already be dealing with funerals and all of the other things that come with the death of a loved one? By undertaking your own version of Swedish Death Cleaning as part of your midlife makeover, you are giving yourself and your family a gift. You get to remember the special moments of your life as you sort through your belongings, and you can even gift things right then and there to the people you want, with the rest of your unwanted goods being donated or tossed accordingly. Your family receive the gift of knowing that they won't have such a huge task when you pass.

I can't stress enough the benefits of taking the time to do a big physical declutter at midlife. As you pare back on the things that tie you to your past, you literally and figuratively make space for your future. Not only will you feel calmer and more focused when you are in your streamlined, orderly home – you will feel lighter and more open to experiences and relationships as your focus moves from what you own, to who you are and who you want to spend time with.

If you have never undertaken a large decluttering project before however, chances are you will feel overwhelmed at the thought of where to begin. Hence I suggest that you follow the following action steps very carefully so that you set yourself up for success. The last thing you want is for complete overwhelm to kick in part way through, leaving you with a mess that is way bigger than your original clutter. Your decluttering exercise might take you weeks or longer as you fit it in around the rest of your life, but be encouraged, it will absolutely be worth the effort!

ACTION STEPS:

- Choose one small space to start with. I usually suggest that people start with the countertop in their bathroom or ensuite. Pop on some party music, set a timer for 20 minutes and get to work!
- Clear every item off the countertop and lay them out on the floor. Group according to type - e.g: shaving related objects; soaps; skin care items; makeup items; hair products etc.
- Once that 20 minute timer goes off, stop what you are doing, grab a drink of water, shake yourself down, then reset for the next 20 minutes. Continue on using the timer until you have completed decluttering and organising this zone.
- Once all of the products are cleared, go through each individual item. Do you use it regularly? Has it expired? Do you have multiples? Divide all of the objects into 3 piles as you sort them: to donate, (although it's pretty unlikely there will be many items to donate from this zone) to toss, and to keep.
- Thoroughly clean the area, and only return necessary essential items to the countertop: for instance, your soap and your toothbrush stand.
- Organise the rest of the items that you have chosen to keep into containers, and store them according to type. I've not mentioned containers or organising until this stage, as it is too easy to disappear into the aisles of pretty containers at K-Mart and simply rearrange your clutter with them once you get home. It's critical

to **remove** as much of the clutter as possible, and once that is done, then you can choose your pretty storage options to suit the space that is left.
- Stand back and admire your clear, sparkling countertop. How do you feel? It's important to take the time to really experience the joy that this small victory gives you. That's the feeling that you want to experience *all* the time in your home and workplace.
- On a list of paper, write out the main hotspots in your home where clutter accumulates. Out of them, choose one zone to tackle per week, (you can change this number according to how large the area is or how much time you have to dedicate to the process.) Using the technique outlined above, work your way through these zones. Notice I haven't said "rooms?" Tackling an entire room – particularly at the beginning of your decluttering process – can be overwhelming, not to mention an absolute nightmare when you are in the sorting phase with everything laid out. Tackling "zones" instead breaks things down and leads to more wins along the way. For instance, zones in your bedroom might be: your wardrobe; your jewellery; under your bed; your ensuite cupboards or drawers; your bedside table. It is far easier to tackle zones when you are also living a busy life, so pin your zone list up somewhere and start ticking them off as they are decluttered.
- Don't forget to take some before and after photos! They will encourage you as you work your way

through your home, and you will feel such a sense of pride when you look at them.

Want some more direction in how to get started with your decluttering process? You can grab my free workbook "10 Hacks to Simplify your Life" here: https://bit.ly/10hacksreport

HACK #8

Declutter your Life – Digital Clutter

> "Digital minimalism is a philosophy that helps you question what digital communication tools (and behaviors surrounding these tools) add the most value to your life. It is motivated by the belief that intentionally and aggressively clearing away low-value digital noise, and optimizing your use of the tools that really matter, can significantly improve your life."
>
> ~ CAL NEWPORT

Computers, phones, apps and programs are meant to make our lives easier. We literally have the world at our fingertips, along with the potential to build wildly profitable businesses, or huge followings for our writing or art – right from the comfort of our own recliner with a laptop on our knees.

We are able to access systems and processes to help us store information, process information and connect instantly with others – so much so that our grandparents would be boggled if they saw it all. Yet despite all of this – we are stressed and overwhelmed, a state that can result in procrastination and lack of productivity.

Have you ever suddenly caught yourself scrolling mindlessly through social media, and realised with horror that you've lost 3 hours of time with nothing to show for it?

Have you found yourself wasting precious minutes trying to wade through the hundreds of emails in your accounts trying to find the one you need?

Or how about those times when you open your laptop and feel a huge weight suddenly settle onto your shoulders as you are immediately confronted with a desktop completely covered in saved files and images?

Digital Clutter has the same impact on you as physical clutter. It's frustrating, embarrassing, soul-sapping and time wasting however, whereas physical clutter might only be an issue in your home, digital clutter can drastically affect your performance in the workplace, regardless of whether you are an employee or an employer. This is bad news on both fronts: if you are an entrepreneur, the distraction caused by clutter can directly affect your income and success. If you are an employee, the time wasted searching for files or being distracted by clutter on your devices, can directly impact your job security when you are seen to be not performing to par.

Digital Clutter might not have been around as long as physical clutter, but it is an issue here to stay and one that we need to learn to manage. When you think about it, most of us grew up hearing our parents tell us to clean our rooms and pick up our toys. I can virtually guarantee however, that those who grew up with computers never heard "clean your desktop, tidy up your files" from their parents! It feels like we have been given access to the tools, but taught none of the rules about how to keep our computers tidy after we have finished playing for the day.

We hear about minimalism in regards to physical clutter. One of the catch cries of minimalists is that the movement is about living with less, as opposed to organising clutter into pretty storage containers. The same rule applies to your digital world. There are apps essential for your work, but we often have so many other apps cluttering our digital space, doing nothing to serve our business or peace of mind. Your computer might be overflowing with files, yet simply organising them will not solve the problem. Organised clutter is still clutter when you can't find what you are looking for, or you get distracted by all the shiny things, or your productivity takes a huge hit – as does your wallet – when you need to pay for more storage to contain all of that digital clutter.

If you are going to ROCK your midlife season, it's important to declutter ALL of your digital devices. As well, it is also critical to prevent the same old habits taking over, so you will need to establish an ongoing set of personal habits that keep you in the drivers seat, and your digital world where it belongs – as a tool to SUPPORT you, not RULE you!

ACTION STEPS:

- Take a good look at your laptop or desk computer – choose the main one that you work from. *How does it make you feel?* Now open your email accounts. (I say accounts as most people have more than one.) Are they full of emails that you don't know what to do with? *How does that make you feel?* Now close your eyes for a minute and visualise what it would look like to see your computer absolutely clear of visual clutter. Lean into that image – *how would that feel?*

  It would feel great wouldn't it? Now hang on to that feeling and let's get started making it a reality. Whenever you feel overwhelmed, shut your eyes and repeat this process – that is the feeling you are after!

- Start with your desktop. Arrange all of your key files in a line down one side of the screen, and add one more to them labelled Miscellaneous. Now click through every other item, one by one. Is it something that you need? If so, file it immediately. Not needed? Send it straight to trash. Unsure? Pop it in the miscellaneous file – *for now!*

- Head into your first email account and follow the same process. Have the most important areas in your life and business labelled as files – including another Miscellaneous file. Click on each email in your inbox and sort accordingly, adding it to the correct file, sending it to the trash or adding it to the miscellaneous folder if you are unsure.

- Once you have finished all of the sorting of your desktop and emails, crank the upbeat music then go back and tackle any miscellaneous folders! You will find it easier to sort the contents of these folders now, as you've been strengthening your "decision muscle" with all of the decisions you have made up to now!
- Now on to your bookmarks! Scroll through your browser bookmarks and delete or group accordingly. You will be amazed at what you discover, (speaking from personal experience here!) Trimming this list right down will make it so much quicker when you are searching for a particular site that is important to you.
- Work your way now through all of your folders, using the file, trash or miscellaneous system. This task alone has the potential to feel overwhelming, so make sure to use the technique of 20 minutes of focussed activity followed by a dance around the room to keep your energy pumping. Just like when you physically declutter your home and work on one zone at a time, apply the same strategy to your files. For example, sort the folders in your dropbox on day 1. Sort the folders in your Google drive on day 2. Sort the files in your email on day 3. You get the idea.
- What small daily habits are you going to put in place to maintain the order in your digital devices that you have worked so hard to declutter and organise? Many people swear by the practice of having an empty inbox at the end of the day. Others ensure that they clear their digital desktop once their work is completed,

exactly the same way that they would clear their physical desktop at the end of their workday. These small habits will be the key to helping you keep that amazing feeling of calm, so that you can focus on the things that *really* matter in your life.

HACK #9
Declutter your Life – Mental Clutter

> "... the stress created by information overload, physical clutter, and the endless choices required from these things can trigger an array of mental health issues like generalised anxiety, panic attacks, and depression ..."
>
> ~ S.J. SCOTT

Congratulations on taking action to clear your physical and digital clutter! If you've have been taking intentional action, I'm sure that you are already feeling lighter, happier and able to focus more on the things that REALLY matter instead of being distracted by the mass of laundry, paperwork and gym gear that has taken over your dining room table or computer desktop. Decluttering doesn't stop there however, as there is one other area that needs to be decluttered urgently if you are truly wanting to ROCK your midlife as well as those years beyond. This area is without a doubt, the most important area to declutter and is one that you will need to strive to keep decluttered every day.

We are talking about decluttering your mind.

The human brain is literally bombarded by enormous amounts of information every second of the day, given that we are constantly receiving information via all of our senses – taste, touch, sight, smell and hearing. Our brain works constantly to process this barrage of information, including filtering it according to whether it thinks the information essential or not. Appropriate signals are then sent to the body to respond accordingly. Scientists believe that we receive approximately 34 gigabytes of information daily, and this sheer volume of information, combined with a brain primed to alert us to danger, means that we live with a certain level of stress every single day.

Living with a base level of stress is perfectly normal. It means our brain is doing its job of sifting through the information it receives to check for any information that might be harmful. When something is discovered, the brain alerts the nervous system which responds accordingly, putting the body into what is commonly known as fight or flight mode. When we get overloaded with information however, this base level of stress increases, meaning that we are now trying to function while our bodies are primed for extreme danger. When we are in this state of stress, hormones including adrenaline and cortisol are released from the adrenal glands, and these affect every organ, priming the body to respond to the danger.

There are numerous physical and emotional reactions that are triggered by this stress response of the body, which can range from mild to debilitating. The intensity of these responses can be affected by our genetics – we are wired this way – or influenced by our mental processes, where we find ourselves stuck in a cycle of increasing stress as our thoughts compound the signals of danger.

Symptoms of a stressed person can range from the mildly uncomfortable, right through to the downright scary – not a state you want to be in if you are to truly ROCK your midlife! Here are some examples:

- Churning stomach
- Diarrhoea
- Dry mouth
- Sweating
- Muscular tensions – especially the jaw, neck and head causing migraines
- Nervousness and anxiousness
- Irritability
- Lack of focus and concentration
- Anger and a short fuse
- Forgetfulness
- Fatigue
- Low mood
- Overwhelm and procrastination
- Overthinking at night time
- Teeth grinding and clenching

- Overeating or undereating
- Increased substance use
- Heart palpitations

Over time, living in a state of chronic or ongoing stress can lead to ...
- Anxiety
- Irritable bowel syndrome, nausea and heartburn issues
- Too much sleep or insomnia
- Headaches, jaw aches and dental issues from grinding and clenching
- Depression
- Ongoing difficulty with concentration
- Ongoing eating disorders and substance abuse
- Weight gain or loss
- Ongoing irritability
- High blood pressure
- Heart issues
- Loss of libido

Hopefully reading this list has reinforced the importance of reducing stress in your life, as if left unchecked – the negative impact on your body can be enormous. Clearing the clutter in your mind is perhaps THE most important thing that you can do to reduce the physical stress response of your body. As many NLP practitioners point out – the brain does not distinguish between real and imaginary thoughts, it processes both the same, hence the clutter in your mind that isn't even true, can be contributing to your stress response.

So how do we accumulate mental clutter? I personally don't know of anyone who would choose to live in a state of stress with all of its physical manifestations, yet so many of us do, and these are some of the ways that mental clutter can start to grow:

- We obsess about something or someone who has wronged us.
- We live in a cluttered environment, contributing to sensory overload that causes our brain to go into overdrive as it tries to process everything.
- We dwell on the negatives in our life.
- We worry about things out of our control.
- We hold on to negative experiences, thinking about them over and over and reliving the negative emotions of hurt, pain, embarrassment and shame.
- We live under the weight of a huge mental list of things that we think we *should* be doing and *should* have achieved.

The common thread that runs through all of these examples?

You.

Your patterns of thinking are the main contributors to your mental clutter, creating a well worn neurological pathway in your brain that you automatically follow every day. Chances are that you are almost completely unaware of an automatic loop of negative thinking occurring non stop as you go about your work. It has become as natural to you as breathing, but it is a pattern that needs to be broken if your body is to have a fighting chance at lowering its level of stress.

Clearing the mental clutter is essential if you want to reinvent or transform your life in any way. It's possibly THE most important thing you can do for yourself at midlife and doing it is basically a pattern interrupt. You are interrupting the thinking patterns that have gotten you to where you are now: overwhelmed, despondent, unable to focus, unproductive, worried and battling chronic health issues.

True reinvention or transformation at midlife can only come about if these negative thought loops cluttering your mind are interrupted and changed. To state it even more bluntly – if you don't take the time to clear your mental clutter, NOTHING in your life will change. If you do the work however, and commit to *continuing* to do the work – you will be creating the space for new thoughts, new dreams, new goals and new experiences, along with a healthier body due to far less stress to carry you through your next season.

Are you ready to start clearing?

ACTION STEPS:

- Mindfulness matters! There is so much information about "mindfulness" out there and whilst some of it can be labelled "woo woo," there are certain techniques firmly rooted in science that I recommend to clients. These enable you to stop the negative thinking and rising anxiety in order to bring you back into the present moment. Doing so means that you can focus fully on the task at hand without the distraction of your busy brain and hyper-alert senses primed for danger. I wrote about one such technique in my first book *21 Hacks to ROCK your Life*. Developed by Jon Kabat-Zinn, a scientist who is considered the father of the modern mindfulness movement, there are numerous variations – including my own – of his method of focused breathing which enables the body's senses to de-escalate from their alert state.

    My years as a professional musician have served me well when it comes to breathing, right from my very first saxophone lesson at aged 12 where I laid on my back with a book on my stomach to understand the principle of diaphragmatic breathing. Not the most auspicious start to my dream of becoming a professional musician, but an exercise that firmly cemented the understanding of diaphragmatic breathing, and one that I used with my own instrumental students and choir members for many years after.

Learning to lower your diaphragm enables you to fill your lungs completely, which in turn counters possible hyperventilation from shallow breathing. Left unchecked, hyperventilation will stimulate your stress hormones, compounding your feelings of anxiety and overwhelm.

Your challenge now is to catch yourself procrastinating. Once you do, check your mental state: *is your brain cluttered and racing with a dozen different thoughts fighting for attention?*

How is your body responding? Is your breathing shallow and rapid? Do you feel anxious? Is your stomach churning?

Follow these steps to calm the body and mind and regain clarity of focus:

1. Step away from the scene. Remove yourself from the physical location where you are feeling stressed – even if just to walk around the corner. If your stress is being triggered by another person – your partner, your teenager, your annoying boss – I suggest that you remove yourself quickly before your mouth kicks in and things escalate to a whole new level of stress!
2. Expand your ribcage, push down your diaphragm and take a 7 second breath in through your nose. Hold for 7 seconds then release through your mouth for 7 seconds.
3. Repeat for at least a minute, focussing on counting the seconds, until you can feel that your stress

levels have dropped and you are feeling calmer.
4. Reconsider the situation that you were in. What is the very first task that you should apply yourself to get through it?
5. Prioritise that in your thinking, then go back and focus *only* on that task until it is completed. This is especially important as you will be training your brain to focus on the task at hand instead of racing all over the pace.

- Daily meditation/prayer. This daily practise is essential as it forces you to calm your racing thoughts and cut through the noise in your head. While the mindfulness technique of step one is a response in the moment, daily prayer / meditation is what will help reinforce the change in your thought loops long term. Find a quiet location where the temperature is not too warm or too cold, and simply close your eyes and pray. Calm all of the thoughts that will be clamouring for attention, and focus on your communication with God. Allow trust to fill you, as trusting that God has heard you means that you don't need to keep anxiously worrying about things over and over – especially those things that you cannot control.
- Do a brain dump. Think of this as a daily decluttering exercise for your mind. Choose a time of day and commit yourself to taking 10 minutes to write out every thought that is in your mind. This act alone can help

lower your anxiety levels, as you are acknowledging the things your brain is trying to alert you to.

Examine this list and put a line through anything outside of your control. Next, put a circle around anything urgent. Transfer these urgent items to your planner, then check the last group – the things you can control, but aren't urgent. Write dates next to these, then add to your yearly planner. This way you have decluttered your mind, dispensing with the need for your brain to hold on to to-do lists, and clearing space instead for creative thinking.

- Find a trusted confidant. Having a trusted friend or family member to talk to is another way of helping you clear your mental clutter. This is especially important for extraverts who process information externally, meaning that they need to talk things out. If you don't have someone in your life like this, turn it around – who can you be that person for? It's like that old saying "if you want friends, you need to be a friend." Become that trusted person for someone else and you will soon find your own confidant. In the meantime however, try journalling. Write out all of your fears and worries, then reframe them right there in your journal. This can be a powerful way of working through what are real concerns, and what are simply lies that your brain has been telling you.
- Create your own "50 posts of awesome" book. No matter how skilled you become at implementing mindfulness techniques or practising your daily

time-out of meditation or prayer – there are still going to be times when negative voices fill your head. It might be that someone has a dig at you which triggers those voices, but chances are, they will simply be your regular friendly gang of negativity that hang out smoking behind the metaphorical school toilets in the back of your brain, telling you that you're not worthy of success, you don't deserve success, you are not talented enough, clever enough, pretty enough, young enough … you know the drill.

We talked about reframing and writing your "I ams" in Hack #6, Filter the Voices, and this time, I'm going to give you another practical tool that you can use right away to demolish your mental gang of naysayers. To start, what is one of the lies you are telling yourself? Let's choose a popular one for people over 40: *I'm too old to start a business*.

The first step is to flip that statement: *I am **not** too old to start a business*. Think of this new statement as a table top which now needs posts to hold it up. Grab your notebook, and the idea is to write 50 – *yes, 50!* – posts to support this statement. Some examples might be:

1. *This is the perfect season in my life for me to start a business as I now have the time I didn't have in my younger years.*
2. *Everything that I have learned through life has helped me grow and be ready right now to start my business.*

3. *I have the knowledge right now to start my business which I never had previously.*

Whenever those negative voices start cluttering up your thinking, pull out your 50 posts book and remind yourself about how awesome you really are!

SECTION 4

PROJECT YOU

"By Failing to prepare, you
are preparing to fail."

~ BENJAMIN FRANKLIN

HACK #10
What Do You Want?

> "Create the highest grandest vision possible for your life, because you become what you believe."
> ~ OPRAH WINFREY

You've probably heard this old saying time and time again: *if you aim at nothing, you'll hit nothing.* Trust me when I say that this statement is just as relevant when it comes to creating a second season of your life that rocks!

You want a life that is full of abundance, laughter, love and purpose?

What does that look like?

How does it feel?

Does the very thought light you up inside?

If you can't picture it or articulate it I can virtually guarantee that you will not ever achieve it!

We've touched on visualisation a few times already, but being able to visualise the future you want is a powerful start to bringing that future to reality. You may not know exactly *how* this future is going to come to fruition, but that's not the issue at this stage.

Without taking the time to do this step repeatedly, you run the risk of wandering aimlessly through your midlife season, living in a reactive mode where external circumstances and other people's agendas shape your path. The problem with living like this however, is that you run the risk of waking up in your 70s and realising that you never achieved YOUR goals. You worked hard at your job, making someone else's goals a reality, but now it is literally too late to achieve those dreams that you had secretly held for your second season.

I don't know about you, but I don't want to live like that – *and I'm speaking from experience here!*

A few years ago, I made the mistake of being swept along by some strong personalities to join a network marketing company they were part of. Initially things were exciting – I was now part of a team with a common goal and I was inundated with meetings and conferences. The shine dulled incredibly quickly however when my own inner voice began protesting, softly at first, but soon becoming a loud, nagging banshee. I was going against my own values when I witnessed women I had introduced to the business having to sit through meetings held by a particularly unbalanced upline.

Almost immediately, I started pulling back, refusing to put myself in situations where this person could have direct input into my life – which unfortunately compounded their attention on me. I heard repeatedly what was being said about me – almost from the minute I had joined – and felt hurt, confused and annoyed at myself. Not only had I put myself in this position, I was also using my weekends – taking time away from my family – to promote someone else's product instead of following my own calling.

The proverbial poop hit the fan when I learned that my closest friend's breast cancer had metastasised and she only had months to live. The reality of her lack of time hit me hard and shone a huge light on the life I was living – and it wasn't the life that I had pictured when I had been dreaming about my next season back in my early forties.

Something had to change, so I left – completely. I handed over my place in the business and took the hit in lack of income. Was it worth it though?

You betcha!

My friend ended up passing away only 6 weeks later, and over the subsequent months, so did 3 other friends. Each death reminded me how life is so fragile and fleeting, and served as a strong reminder that I owed it to myself – AND the people I wanted to serve – to live with integrity and purpose.

I decided that I would no longer allow other people's agendas to determine what I do or where I put my energy – regardless of how well meaning they might be. The first step I took in reclaiming my life was to go back and clearly picture *exactly* what the life I wanted to live looked like.

And now it is your turn to do likewise.

ACTION STEPS:

- Find a quiet place and close your eyes. Let yourself dream while you ponder these questions:
  1. *If you had no boundaries, what would you do?*
  2. *Where would you live?*
  3. *How would you look?*
  4. *How would you feel?*
  5. *Who would be in your life?*
- Don't get hung up on details! When you are picturing your life in your next season, the idea is simply to create a real, tangible picture, not to worry about the details of how you are going to get there. Repeat step 1 and let those dreams be even bigger!
- Create a vision board to represent *all* of the aspects of the life you want. This can be a digital board, or you can take your time to create a physical board. Make it as artistic and creative as you want, while ensuring that it clearly covers every aspect of your dream life.
- Take time every day after your meditation / prayer time, to picture the life you want. Train your brain as well as your soul, to *know* and to *feel* exactly what you are aiming for.
- Determine right now that you are not going to be swayed by other people's agendas. By all means listen when opportunities are presented to you, but learn to put emotion aside, and go through the exercise of comparing the opportunity to the picture of the life that you want to create. If the opportunity and the image match – go for it! If not – walk away.

> Time is not guaranteed – if ever you were going to bring your dreams to life, it needs to be now!

HACK #11
What Don't You Want?

> "You'll never know who you are unless you shed who you pretend to be."
>
> ~ VIRONIKA TUGALEVA

While the first step to creating a purposeful life in your next season is clearly knowing what life you want, the second is being absolutely clear about what you *don't* want. Not having a clear picture of the person you want to become, the life you want to live and the life that you *don't want to live*, means that you may find yourself in a situation like I experienced – living out someone else's agenda.

Let's dig a little deeper into my experience and how I found myself in a role that I had never intended to be in … I knew what I wanted in my second season of life:

- *I wanted to be my own boss.*
- *I wanted to have flexibility in my work times.*
- *I wanted regular, scalable income.*

- *I wanted a positive network of entrepreneurial women that I could learn from and relate to.*
- *I wanted to improve my health naturally (given that I live with a chronic pain condition.)*
- *I wanted to help other women create purposeful businesses that would support them and their families.*

At face value, the network marketing business I joined ticked everything on this list, and you may well be asking what my problem was. On the surface, I had the flexible hours, the scaleable income, the positive network (generally speaking), ways to improve my health and the supposed answer to helping other women's financial needs. However, as I have already outlined in the previous hack, the initial excitement died out very quickly and I soon found myself:

- *Uncomfortable when what I witnessed and personally experienced crossed my personal values.*
- *Hurt at the back stabbing.*
- *Embarrassed professionally when I buckled under pressure and advertised the products on my business pages and in my newsletters.*
- *Financially drained when I had to purchase extra amounts of products to ensure that my uplines and myself qualified for our rank payouts each month.*
- *Angry at myself for getting swept up into the madness in the first place.*

Had I been clear on what I *didn't* want in this next season of life, I would have seen the red flags right away when the offer to join the team was made. More importantly, I would have *acknowledged* those flags and trusted my gut which was telling me at the time that this wasn't the right path for me!

Knowing what you *don't want* is just as important as knowing what you *do want*. It prevents you from repeating mistakes, blindly following someone else's agenda and accepting far less than what you are worth in your job, your relationships and your life in general.

Whilst I don't recommend that you focus on what you don't want every day, it *is* important to take the time and write that list down at least once, so you can use this description as a lens through which you can examine any new opportunity or invitation.

ACTION STEPS:

- Find a quiet place and think back over the many experiences you have had up to this point of time. What were great experiences? What were not so great and what were downright awful experiences?
- Honing in on the negative experiences, grab a pencil and paper and write down the list of learnings you received from going through them. The idea here is to not berate yourself or get angry at yourself, but rather to acknowledge that there were lessons learned from going through these experiences. Even the toughest times in our life can produce learnings and insights.
- Bearing these lessons in mind, write down what you *do not want* in your next season of life. Some examples might be:
    1. I do not want to work for a boss any longer.
    2. I do not want someone else dictating what hours I work.
    3. I do not want to be in a relationship where I am treated like a second class citizen.
    4. I do not want to earn a salary that is so low that I am always struggling to pay my bills.
    5. I do not want to sell something I don't believe in.

You get the idea!

- Pop this list in the back of your yearly planner and refer to it every time that you are presented with an opportunity that appears to tick all of the boxes on your list of what you DO want in life. Consider your DON'T WANT list as your last line of defence that prevents you from jumping into something exciting and new, without having done your due diligence.

You've spent so many years of your life compromising on many of your dreams – don't allow yourself to compromise any more as you head into your midlife season!

HACK #12
Research

> "Research is what I'm doing when I don't know what I'm doing."
>
> ~ WERNHER VON BRAUN

Now that you have determined what you do and do not want going forward, things get exciting as you now get to start the process that I particularly love – RESEARCH!

This is where you get to explore all of your interests. For instance, let's say that being an artist has been one of the dreams you've toyed with now and then – start researching it! Be like a curious child and ask yourself lots of questions. What style of painting do you like? Who are the artists already working in that style? What courses or workshops are available? What is the time commitment and the financial investment?

While doing this research process, you need to keep your inner critic well and truly gagged and tied up in the corner. Her negative talk of *"you're too old, it's too late to start anything new,"* yada, yada has no place here. You are simply gathering information, not making life changing decisions on a whim and this period of research needs to be free of any self-limiting thoughts so that you can fully explore *all* of the possibilities for your next season.

Want to start your own business?
- *Cool! What product or service are you thinking of?*
- *Are there businesses already out there with a similar offering?*
- *What are their websites like?*
- *What are their social media sites like?*
- *Do they offer free giveaways? Grab them and get on their mailing list.*
- *What do you like about their business model?*
- *What don't you like?*
- *What would you do differently?*

How about writing your first book?
- *What genre appeals to you?*
- *Who are your favourite authors?*
- *How long are their books?*
- *Have they self published or been published by a traditional publisher?*
- *Are there courses you can take or writing groups you can join?*
- *What are their newsletters and social media like?*

Do you see how fun this can be? By giving yourself permission to be curious and explore with no self-imposed boundaries, you might be amazed at what you discover. Even better, you may well find that you ignite a spark of excitement as your next season starts to take shape in your mind.

That November afternoon when I sat on my deck watching my daughter excitedly opening envelope after envelope of university offers, my stomach churned with the mix of emotions that I was feeling. On the one hand, I was so happy for her. She had worked so hard, juggling course work, a huge training schedule, international competitions, a part time coaching job, music lessons, band gigs and general teenage life, and I was SO proud of what she had achieved. On the other hand though, I was freaking: *What the heck do I do now?*

Being an introvert, I started asking myself all of the same questions I have been asking you. I asked myself what I *did* want to do, I identified what I *didn't* want to do, and then I tossed around a dozen different ideas and asked myself over and over *what if?*

What if I got a regular 9–5 job?

What if I went back to teaching?

What if I went back to university to do postgraduate study?

What if I tried something completely different?

Soon, two different pathways started to form once I clarified exactly what I did and didn't want in my next season:

I didn't want to go back into teaching, (6 years of homeschooling tends to change your philosophy of education!)

I didn't want to work a 9-5.

I wanted to be able to develop my own business.

And most importantly, I wanted to work in a job that allowed me to help people.

These two options might seem a bit odd to you, but these option are what I came up with following my research: a funeral director or a personal trainer.

So you might be thinking me a tad strange at the moment, but the reality was that both of these roles met the criteria of what I did and didn't want to pursue in my next season. In fact if anything, I was more suited to the funeral director role, having already presided over two funerals a few years earlier and having been in ministry in the past. As for the personal training course, there was the slightly awkward fact that I was *very* overweight and hadn't darkened a gym door – other than to watch my daughter compete – for at least 10 years!

Taking the time to do the research set me on the path to where I am today. As I dug deeper into each role, I discovered that one was better suited to me in regards to flexibility, which was one of the key things that I desired. I also discovered that the study for one of these roles could be done relatively close to my home, that I could apply for a government funded student loan, and that I could eventually launch my own business with the skills I would learn and some experience under my belt.

I went on to became a personal trainer, which positively impacted not only my health and fitness, but also my family's. They started exercising more, (my daughter and husband ended up competing in different bodybuilding classes) and our family grew healthier and stronger, as did the numerous clients I had the privilege of working with over the following years.

The process of launching and growing my personal training business, utilising the power of Facebook Groups to expand online, eventually morphed into my creating a movement empowering midlife women. I was soon featured in a 6 page spread of a national magazine, made various radio, TV and podcast appearances, hosted my own events, workshops and podcast, published my own books and spoke at numerous international conferences, both in real life and virtually.

And now I help other midlife women create their own purposeful lives and businesses, all because …

I didn't go back into teaching.

I didn't go into a 9–5.

I indeed developed my own business.

And most importantly, I created a business that did – and still does – enables me to help people.

ACTION STEPS:

- Go back through the previous hacks of this book and write a definitive list of what you do and what you don't want to do in your next season. Whether you are talking about a complete career / life change like I did, launching a side hustle, or wanting to pursue a long-held dream of writing, painting, horse-riding ballroom dancing *or whatever* – you will need this list.
- Once you have itemised your want / don't want list, write down the list of choices that you have. Some of these might feel like the most ridiculous dreams compared to your current reality, but remember that your inner critic has been gagged, so add them to your list!

  If you are an introvert like myself, chances are that you will figure out your options in your head. If you are an extravert however, you will need to process this aloud, so find a trusted friend who won't judge or dismiss your ideas as far-fetched and unrealistic, and bounce your thoughts off them until you have defined your list of options.
- Now comes the fun part! Write down your list of curious questions for each option you want to investigate, on a separate piece of paper. If you are a real methodical type, you might prefer to do this on a spreadsheet. Give yourself a few hours to research with no interruptions and start with a broad Google search for your first option. Referring back to your questions, you'll soon start discovering all sorts of

interesting information. Let yourself go down the rabbit holes and if you need more time to explore, take it – especially if you are contemplating a major life change or transformation. Better to have explored all of your opportunities before committing yourself to something – particularly if you need to invest in training or equipment.

- Once you have completed your research, you should have a very clear idea of what you are going to pursue in your next season. Sit on this for a few days and see how it feels. If you feel uneasy, go back, ask yourself some more questions and do some more research. If you are feeling excited – woohoo! You are on your way to creating your next season!

HACK #13
Who Will You Need?

> "I'm not the smartest fellow in the world, but I sure can pick smart colleagues."
>
> ~ FRANKLIN D. ROOSEVELT

I mentioned in the last hack how introverts like myself tend to process information internally, which can sometimes be a surprise to those around who haven't been privy to the researching and weighing up of options. My family were certainly caught off guard when I announced to them out of the blue how I was going to return to school in order to become a personal trainer – oh, and that I had an interview with the New Zealand Institute of Sport the very next day!

I personally wouldn't recommend this method, given that no-one lives in a vacuum and your decisions always affect others, however, thankfully my family are well aware of what I can be like! Once I was accepted into the course, it wasn't just my life that changed – my entire family's did as they adjusted to my suddenly not being so available. I was either training at the gym, in classes or doing my study and assignments late into the night.

Things changed at home, especially – heaven forbid – when I was unable to keep up cooking every night! The family had to step up and pitch in, whereas for the previous 6 years, they had had a full-time mother, taxi driver, chef and housekeeper at their beck and call. Chances are, once you begin to put action to making your dreams a reality, you will be changing your home and possibly your workplace dynamic too. Whether it is the shift in your time availability and priorities, or the fact that you yourself have changed with a new confidence and spring in your step – those closest to you in your daily life will need to adjust too.

The way to make the transition smoother for them and for you? To include some of them in your dream team. I wrote about the concept of a dream team in my original book *21 Hacks to ROCK your Life!* Having a team of key people who have your success in mind is an incredibly powerful factor in helping you make your dream a reality at midlife, and regardless of whether you are an introvert or an extravert – we all need one!

The concept of a dream team does not include every provider of particular services you might use. For instance, I have used editors and printers for my books, however none of these people are part of my dream team. Those positions are reserved for people who not only have the skills and knowledge that I need, but are people who know me, and who I know and trust.

Dream teams aren't set in concrete but can change over time as some members move out of your life and others join. For instance, when I was studying to become a personal trainer, my dream team consisted of my husband, my nutritionist, my personal trainer / lecturer, a close friend that I made on the course and my closest girlfriend who was also returning to study as part of her midlife transition.

Over time that changed as I graduated and took a job in a gym, which soon morphed into my own personal training business, which morphed again into my online coaching, podcasting, writing and speaking business. These days, my dream team still contains my husband, as well as some key friends who are professional speakers, my business coach and my mastermind coaches. As well, I have 3 key women in different countries who I can reach out to when needed.

Notice that my husband is in both groups? Being married to a fiery Italian, I discovered very early in our marriage that we needed to be open and in agreement with each other if our relationship was to last. He has been my number 1 supporter for over 30 years now, and will always and rightfully be part of my team, as anything I put my hand to directly affects him too. The precious girlfriend who was like my sister and a constant member of my earlier dream team for many years, went on to earn her degree in counselling and made a difference to many lives, before she died of cancer on the morning of my son's wedding in 2019. My first 21 Hacks book is dedicated to her. Were she here today, she also would still be part of my dream team.

Having a dream team can often be the difference between *having* a dream and actually *reaching* that dream. A great dream team will:
- *Hold you accountable to achieving your goals.*
- *Challenge you.*
- *Cheer for you and commiserate with you.*
- *Advise you.*
- *Have faith in you when you have none for yourself.*

ACTION STEPS:

- Who are the people who have been part of your "unofficial" dream team to date? Write their names in a list.
- Out of these names, circle those who you want as members of your official dream team in your next season.
- If you feel that your dream team doesn't really understand you or your business, can you find people who do, and see if you can book coffee and a chat with them?
- If there is absolutely no one you personally know who can be part of your dream team – who do your friends know? Ask for introductions if need be. Find highly skilled people and search "around them" as well in case they are too busy.
- People are busy, so don't be offended if someone says that they don't have the time to support you. If in doubt, grab a friend or two and ask them who **they** know. Have them introduce you to this person and start building a relationship.

SECTION 5

READY TO LAUNCH

"Be fearless in the pursuit of
what sets your soul on fire."

~ UNKNOWN

HACK #14

Plan

"Our goals can only be reached through a vehicle of a plan, in which we must fervently believe, and upon which we must vigorously act. There is no other route to success."

~ PABLO PICASSO

This is where things start to get both extremely exciting and extremely scary all at the same time. You've completed your self audit, allowed yourself to dream, let go of the past, filtered all of the voices, *really* listened to your own, decluttered your life to create space, determined what you do and don't want to do, done your research and worked out who you will want in your dream team ... NOW *you get to put pen to paper and start working on a plan to bring those dreams to life!*

It's a funny thing though. This is the step that I find can separate the people who just *talk* about their dreams from the people who actually bring their dreams to *life*. People will attend workshop after workshop, watch webinar after webinar and take course after course on challenging their inner critic, on writing out their dreams, on vision boards, on *all the things* – but never go any further than that.

Writing out your plan is a definitive action in itself. You are no longer thinking "what if" but instead, are moving into a state of expectation and belief as you put pen to paper. Your plan might be super detailed or just a broad outline, depending what kind of planner you are. The fact remains though: by writing your plan down, you will have taken the first concrete step towards bringing your dream to life.

So where to start?

Whenever I work with a client, the process we take is to clearly identify their desired end result and reverse engineer the steps from there.

You've already done the following exercise, however now that you have identified what you *really* want to do in your next season, it's time to do it again so you can clearly visualise yourself achieving that goal:

- Close your eyes and picture yourself having reached your new goal. You might be envisioning yourself leaner and fitter, or in a wonderful, loving new relationship, or succeeding in your new business, or holding your brand new, best selling book, or standing in front of your own successful art exhibition – *or even all of the above!*
- Hold that vision firmly in your mind and lean

in to how you *feel*. Remember that emotions help anchor that image more firmly in your subconscious. How do you look? Where are you? What can you hear, taste and smell?

This image – along with those feelings of confidence, elation and happiness – is your end game, and the plan that you write out now will become the roadmap to help you get there. This plan will also be the thing that separates you from being a frustrated dreamer to becoming the person you envisage – full of confidence, elation and happiness at having achieved your desired end result.

There is no "one size fits all" when it comes to writing your plan. Some people prefer to fill in a digital spreadsheet that itemises every step, along with projected dates of completion. Others prefer a large visual form of planning such as a hand drawn mind map with lots of colours. Choose whichever style works best for you, remembering that the *content* of the plan is the critical thing here, not how you choose to write it out.

ACTION STEPS:

I always recommend that clients adopt the S.M.A.R.T goals framework (Specific, Measurable, Achievable, Relevant, and Time-Bound) when creating their plans, so your first step is to grab a large piece of paper and draft your responses to the following questions as we work our way through the acronym. Once you have completed this draft, you can then transfer your results to your preferred planning template and calendar.

S: Specific. The picture that you created in your head at the beginning of this hack is the starting point for your plan, and your first job is to describe the *specifics* of that end goal:

What do you want to achieve?

When do you want to have achieved it by?

What will it look like?

How will you know that you have achieved it?

You need to be extremely detailed with this description, so keep revisiting the mental image you created while you are writing things down. For example, if your goal in this next season is to write a best selling book, just writing "I want to publish a best selling book by December 2021" is not nearly specific enough. Instead, you could write this:

"By December 7th 2021, I will have uploaded my fictional cozy mystery book of 75,000 words to my new AMAZON author account." You can see how the second description is far more detailed, adding the specifics of date, genre, word count, distributor and also making it clear that you will be self-publishing. Write your end goal now, using lots of specifics.

M: Measurable. If you have clearly written out the specifics of your end-goal, you will already have a good idea about how to measure your progress along the way.

In our example of publishing a novel, we have a date and a word count to measure against: December 7th and 75 000 words. It will be obvious whether you hit that date and word target or not. "Measurable" doesn't just refer to the end result however!. It's important to break down the steps you need to progress though in order to meet that time and word count goal. By ensuring that each of these progress steps are also measurable, you will be able to identify if you are on track to achieving your overarching goal. This is where the research you undertook in hack #12 will come into play as you already know what you need to do to reach your goal.

Measurable steps in your plan to publish your 75,000 word novel by December 7th might include the following:
a) Write 11,000 words each month from February through to August.
b) Send the manuscript to the editor on September 1st, check feedback, re-write then

check again until all editing is completed by October 20th.
c) While the manuscript is with the editor, complete the dedication and acknowledgements by September 10th so that they are ready for the second editor read through.
d) Complete all artwork and apply for the IBSN numbers by October 20th.
e) Send off the edited manuscript, artwork and inside cover matter to be formatted by October 31st etc.

There are many more steps here but you get the idea. Each step I have listed is easily measured by date and by result. Now break down your goal into the measurable steps that you will need to take to achieve it.

A: Achievable. There are plenty of Instagram memes out there to remind us that our goals should be so big that they scare us. I certainly agree with the premise behind this thought, as I truly believe that we are capable of achieving way more than we give ourselves credit for. When it comes to this stage of the game though, when we are preparing our roadmap to help us reach that goal – we need to bridge the gap between our lofty dreams and our making them real. In other words, our steps need to help us *achieve* our goal, and that means ensuring all of those measurable mini-goals that we just listed are also *achievable*. Sure, there will be growth involved in reaching these goals, but if your mini-goals along the way are simply too hard to achieve, you will set yourself up to fail and each time you miss one, you will be chipping away at the hope you held of making your dream a reality and rocking your midlife season. Chip one too many times, and you run the risk of your confidence being completely shattered.

Go back through your list of Measurable goals now and ensure that they are also achievable.

R: Relevant. All of the mini-goals you create in your roadmap to your big goal need to be *relevant*. It goes without saying that including a mini-goal of learning to ride a horse will not be relevant to your big audacious midlife goal of publishing a 75,000 word novel on December 7th, *unless* you need to know about how to ride a horse for the book! Each of your mini goals should be specific, measurable, achievable and relevant to your overarching goal.

T: Time-bound. We touched on this when we discussed specific and measurable goals, but in some cases, the mini-goals may not have a time connected to them, in which case it is important to assign one. Who knows someone – *maybe even yourself?* – who was going to write and publish a novel 5 years ago, and is still only half way through writing the first draft? I know that I have let myself down on occasions over the years when I didn't meet personal goals I had set myself – and that was generally due to my not putting an absolute deadline on it.

By nature, I hate feeling pinned down and a full diary of appointments makes me shudder, yet I also know that when I have a deadline, my work gets done. Even writing this book was a battle between my choosing to do easier activities like binge watch Netflix or YouTube, or choosing to actually push through the resistance and write! It's ironic how even when you actually *like* the activity you are meant to be doing – in this case writing – how much your brain will still distract you! This book, just like my previous books, is only written because I put a hard deadline in place and made myself meet it.

Was it easy?

Nope!

Was it always fun to write?

Not at all!

Am I glad that I completed it though?

Without a doubt!

Go through all of the mini-goals that you have listed, and carefully estimate the time constraints you will need to put on each step in order to achieve your main goal. Adjusting the timing of your roadmap will be one of the most important things you can do to ensure that you keep momentum, without pushing so hard that you can't meet your deadlines and give up altogether.

Putting it together. You should now be able to articulate your main goal far more succinctly than you were able to in the first action step and it's time to summarize your big, audacious midlife goal:

> *By* [date}, *I will complete my goal of* [objective]. *I will use these steps,* [itemise your key mini-goals] *and when I achieve my goal I will feel* [emotion].

Write this sentence out at the top of your planning template, and stick it in places where you are guaranteed to see it each day, for example, at the top of your bathroom mirror, in the front cover of your planner, or on the home screen of your computer. Doing so will remind you every day of what you have committed to achieving, when it is going to be achieved and how amazing you are going to feel.

HACK #15

Setting up for Success

> "Success is a state of mind. If you want success, start thinking of yourself as a success."
>
> ~ DR JOYCE BROTHERS

My hope by this stage of the book is that you are not feeling overwhelmed by the planning exercise of the last hack, but are instead excited about launching into your next season. If you have followed through all of the action steps, you will have in your hand something so many people don't bother creating: your very own personalised roadmap that lays out the *exact* steps you need to take in order to reach your goal.

Isn't that exciting?

When you started reading this book, you might have held a vague idea of what you wanted to do in your next season. Now however, you've not only dreamed about the possibilities, you've actually put pen to paper and created your own personal blueprint. All the guesswork has been thrown out the window as you now know *exactly* what you need to do.

Then why is it that so many other people at this stage still fail to achieve their goals?

You are in the minority with what you have already achieved to this point: You've taken time out to truly reflect on where you are at, where you've been and what you want going forward. You've identified your big audacious dream and reverse engineered it, creating SMART goals to formulate your personal roadmap to success. *Congratulate yourself for valuing YOU enough to complete the planning process thus far!*

There is still another step however, (*you knew you weren't done, right?*) It's critical now that you set yourself up for success! This can mean a myriad of things – many of which we have already touched on – but all are essential to help you stay focussed on reaching each and every one of those mini goals in your blueprint in a timely fashion.

In the years that I worked in a large body building gym in South Auckland as a personal trainer, I saw hundreds of people coming and going. In the earlier years when I worked shifts as a gym instructor, one of my roles was to undertake an introductory assessment of new members. During this meeting, we would discuss their goals, measure their body fat, weight and fitness ability and create a personal plan that would help them reach their overarching goal – be that changing their body composition, competing in a triathlon, powerlifting or bodybuilding competition or simply working out 3 times a week and living a healthier lifestyle.

These assessments were always followed up with an appointment to walk these members through their new program. I would show them everything from where to fill their drink bottle, how to operate a treadmill, to how to lift a dumbbell safely. If I was to guess, I would have to say that 99% of the walk throughs I conducted would conclude with the new member smiling and feeling confident about following their new program. We would book a date for a follow up appointment and more often than not, this new member wouldn't leave right away, but turn around and head straight back onto the gym floor to confidently try the machines for themselves.

Then the season changed.

Or the clocks were turned back from daylight savings.

Or life in general happened, and these excited new members started missing appointments …

Their gym visits became more infrequent and they would look a bit sheepish when greeted as they entered the building. Eventually they stopped coming at all and became yet another gym donor, paying an automated weekly fee until their contract ran out.

I tell you this story not to make fun of these people, as for many years, I was one of them. I had barely set foot in a gym for 10 years prior to my choosing to train to become a personal trainer, but before then, I had donated to many gym owner's bank accounts as I tried the different gyms in my area. I always started with a bang, (usually involving tears in my assessment when I was weighed and measured – an act that frightened more than a few young PTs over the years!) Each time, I decided that this time was going to be **the** time when I actually followed through and changed my woeful state of health and fitness.

And then something would happen.

I would miss a couple of sessions, then embarrassed, I would and try to slink in unnoticed, until eventually I'd stop going at all. I'd try to ignore the shame I felt about letting myself down yet again and wasting money that my family could have used.

In both of these cases, there was a personal roadmap in place which if followed to the letter, would virtually guarantee results.

Indeed, both myself and the new members that I looked after a decade later knew *exactly* what we needed to do, along with how many times a week we needed to do it.

We knew *exactly* how long we needed to rest between sets and how to perform the exercises safely.

As well, we had all been given sound lifestyle advice, (eat healthy, drink lots of water and get lots of sleep etc) yet we still faltered and gave up before even meeting the first milestone of a repeat assessment and program adjustment one month later.

One month! That is all we had to last, yet I saw countless people not make this first milestone – myself included in those earlier years. On the other hand though, I saw a smaller group of members having the opposite experience – as I did myself that year I began my studies to be a personal trainer. This smaller group turned up day after day. They followed their program to the letter, gradually increasing their weights, upping the intensity of their cardio and implementing their lifestyle changes. I witnessed clients lose in excess of 40 kilograms, build muscle, completely overhaul their lifestyle and confidence and meet their goals of competing on stages – including my own husband who competed in 4 bodybuilding competitions for the first time at the age of 53, winning nationals in one of the federations.

What was the difference between those new members who fell by the wayside in their first month, as opposed to those who didn't only stick with it, but went on to smash their goals out of the park?

What was the difference in my behaviour those many times I wasted gym memberships, compared to the year where I went back to school to become a personal trainer and graduated at the top of the class, as well as fitter and 18 kg lighter?

The difference was simple – those that achieved their goals did so because they had *set themselves up for success.*

Having your own roadmap with all of the mini-goals listed that need to be achieved in order to reach your big goal, plays a massive part in the equation of success. However, each of those gym members – along with myself back in the day – all had one of those roadmaps. Our success was virtually guaranteed if we stuck with the plan, yet so many of us didn't even last a few weeks, despite the financial sting of seeing money deducted from our account each month.

Taking the time to *set yourself up for success* is the secret sauce to you following through on the actions you identified as important enough to list in your roadmap. How that looks exactly, is as individual as each goal and roadmap, however there are some common actions you can apply in order to set you up for success in reaching your goal.

ACTION STEPS:

- Plan each week in advance! It sounds an obvious thing to do, yet how many of us take the time on a Saturday or Sunday afternoon to *really* examine the commitments we have coming up in the week ahead? People who succeed in ticking off completed goals each week are almost always the ones who thought ahead and planned their time in advance, leaving nothing to chance. Remember our example goal of writing 11000 words a month? There is no way that this goal will ever be met unless there is *time scheduled* into your weekly planning!
- Treat your goal as a non negotiable appointment. If your boss had booked you for two regular meetings every week, would you stand him up again and again? Of course not – not if you wanted to keep your job! So many of us are guilty of treating our booked meetings with others as set in concrete – totally immovable. However those promises made to ourselves – to exercise, to write, to paint, to build our new business – are broken as soon as something else pops up.

    No more! It's time to honour your own commitments with the same respect you honour your commitments with your boss or other people. If you can't establish this practise from the get go – you will struggle to ever achieve those milestone goals that you are aiming for on the road to your big end goal.

- Plan and prepare! The only way that I broke my habit of donating to the gym was by using the same routine that my husband later adopted, helping him transform from unfit, overweight and near death after post surgical infection, to a national bodybuilding champion.

Our not so secret routine?

Taking the time to plan ahead and prepare each night.

We would both have our gym clothes ready, (in my case, who wants to look for matching socks at 3.30 am?) as well as our keys, gym bag and water bottles which were waiting by the door. In my husband's case, a protein shake, breakfast, lunch and snacks were also packed. We got in the habit of cooking enough at dinner to feed us both for lunch the following day, and we would prep all of our food and snacks while we cleaned up after our meal, so that it didn't feel like yet another chore.

Let's say that one of your midlife goals is to write a book. You've worked out that you will need to meet a word count each day in order to complete the project, so how can you help yourself ensure that sitting down and writing those words becomes a regular non-negotiable appointment with yourself? Some ideas might be: keep a spreadsheet tracking your words for each day in view; have a time slot blocked out in your calendar for writing: have all devices offline during that dedicated writing time.

What if you dream of launching a business? What can you do to find time and maximise your productivity while still working a regular job? Some ways you could set yourself up for success to achieve this goal could be: setting your alarm an hour earlier than usual each morning; pre-scheduling and automating any social media or other regular online tasks; limiting your evening Netflix viewing.

Setting yourself up for success means that you are not *talking* about your goal. Instead, you are taking very real action, and in doing so, you will discover that you are able to adhere to your roadmap with a commitment and focus that you have possibly never experienced before.

HACK #16
Get the Family Buy-In

> "The bond that links your true family is not one of blood, but of respect and joy in each other's life."
>
> ~ RICHARD BACH

If you are an introvert like me, your family may well have been taken by surprise with what you want to achieve in your next season. Not because you have been intentionally keeping secrets, but as we said earlier, due to you processing much of your decision making internally as is the case for most introverts. If you are an extravert however, chances are that your family is well aware of *what* you are thinking, *why* you are thinking it, and every little detail in between as you have probably shared your thinking process with them over and over and over!

Neither approach is right or wrong – they are just different – but it helps if you can explain clearly what has been going on so that your family can understand and be supportive of the process.

Having your family "buy-in" to your dreams and goals for your next season is important if you are to keep your relationships solid as you transition from the person you were to the person that you want to become.

Popular psychology might preach that it's all about you being you, and everyone else be damned if they don't accept your new persona. In the real world however, I've discovered that most women aren't quite so eager to throw aside every one of their close relationships in order to chase their dreams. What's more, my own experience has shown me that dream chasing and family stability don't need to be mutually exclusive.

Transitioning into the person that you want to become at midlife is often akin to "coming home" to the woman who has pushed aside her own goals and aspirations in order to put her family first throughout the first half of her life. Finding or "rediscovering" herself is a concept that many midlife women explore when they find themselves with time to think – something they didn't have the time to do a decade ago when they were in the throes of child and teen rearing / wrangling.

"Finding yourself" doesn't have to mean walking out on your relationship and travelling to far flung countries a la *Eat, Pray, Love* either. Trust me when I say that it *is* possible to go through this process of self discovery without destroying your family, and the woman who manages to do so is often the one that finds herself years down the road content with who she has become, as she juggles her new grandchild on one knee whilst running her business from the laptop on her other knee.

For others though, the midlife self-discovery coincides with the turmoil of leaving or losing significant partnerships and this makes having the support of family – be that your blood family, or your family of choice – extremely important. If every area of your life is in flux, it will be so much more difficult to do the work needed to bring your dreams and goals to life. Having a "soft place to land" – a group of people who love and accept you for the messy, imperfect person that you are – is an essential part of your midlife journey.

ACTION STEPS:

- Have you been dreaming about your next season, wondering what you would like to do and who you would like to become? Maybe you are already at the research stage, but are yet to let your family know what you are exploring. Can I suggest that now is the time to let them in?

    I know that I am not the best example, being the introvert who sprung it on the family that my PT interview was the very next day, however their buy-in *was* important and I asked them for their backing. Letting my family know my thoughts, the direction that I wanted to take and my fears about launching into this new future was nothing but liberating. Their support of my decision made the entire journey into the unknown feel much more achievable and I highly recommend that you do likewise and give your closest inner circle the chance to "buy in" to your new season too.

- Feel like your family is not "getting it?" My suggestion here is that you find someone who has gone before you. Is there another woman you know who has changed her trajectory at midlife to walk a path that is in alignment with her values and passions? What suggestions does she have from her own experience, and can she and her partner share their wisdom with your partner and family?

    Often families will be hesitant at supporting you due to their fear of the unknown as opposed to

any disbelief or disapproval of what you are doing. Meeting someone who has successfully embarked on a similar journey will encourage them to be more supportive of you.
- Do your best to reassure your partner in particular that whilst you are growing and evolving – you are still committed to your marriage and family. Keeping your family unit stable while you explore and evolve will mean you are able to focus on what you are learning and transitioning into, secure in the knowledge that you still have your safe place to land. Neglecting your family unit at this time will negatively affect your own journey, when you find yourself suddenly needing to focus on repairing new fractures in your relationships instead of fully appreciating this time of growth.

SECTION 6

LIFT OFF!

"Action is the foundational key to all success."

– PABLO PICASSO

HACK #17
Ditch the Perfectionism!

> "At its root, perfectionism isn't really about a deep love of being meticulous. It's about fear. Fear of making a mistake. Fear of disappointing others. Fear of failure. Fear of success."
>
> ~ MICHAEL LAW

Perfectionism can easily kill your growth, your courage and your new venture. In my decades of experience working primarily with women, I speak with authority when I state that we really are prone to this behaviour! Unfortunately though, when you believe that your work is not "perfect enough," you will hesitate to act. Please hear me when I say this: if you have a dream or goal at midlife that you want to make real, the clock is ticking honey! It's time to stop waiting until things are "perfect" and time to get things **done!**

There is an observation I hear from midlifers almost

every single day: *the years feel like they are flying by faster than ever.* Those "big" birthdays that include a 0 at the end bring this revelation even closer to home, and it is a very rare person who reaches this age without some level of introspection about how they have lived and what they have achieved to this point.

Women who are mothers go through this crisis more than once. Not only do they have to face the march of time and what they personally have or have not achieved, they also face very real milestones in their family life that also define their roles.

Obvious examples of family milestones are when your babies start school, when your last primary schooler starts high school and the big one – when your young adults leave the nest to go to college, to travel the world, or to work and live elsewhere. This last family milestone is particularly poignant as it affects the main caregiver – generally the mother – in such a profound way.

I've already shared my story of how my own impending empty nest sent me into an entirely new career trajectory that led to my now connecting with literally thousands of women online and speaking in numerous international conferences and summits. Throughout these years however, I battled something so familiar to many women, which could have prevented me from ever speaking my message in the public arena: the trait of perfectionism.

But my branding isn't right!

Shouldn't I hold back from posting on social media when this isn't consistent?

I'm worried that my books aren't good enough!

Maybe I should have held off publishing for another 12 months to triple check that everything I've written is perfect!

I don't know about you, but there are NO times whatsoever that I can recall creating something that I considered to be completely "prefect!"

Waiting until you have something perfect, instead of launching once things are working – be that your new business, blog, novel, artwork or *whatever* – means that you will rob yourself AND those who follow you from receiving what you *do* have to offer.

The lesson to be learned around perfectionism is that there is virtually *always* something that you could do better. There comes a point however, where you need to step away from your baby – be it a book, an artwork, a work project or whatever – and release it to the world. Spending countless months of refining and perfecting your work is only covering up something far deeper: fear.

Hidden behind that desire for perfection is a fear of being seen and being judged, and this fear can cripple your progress on achieving your midlife goals. If you don't reign your perfectionism, you will find that yet another decade has passed with you not achieving the dream that you said was so important to you, until one day, you wake up in your 80s and it's too late.

The remedy to perfectionism? This may sound odd, but in my experience, the remedy is self-discipline. Self-discipline will enable you to put down your tools once something has been completed, checked and done. The self-discipline to stop and put your work out to the world will help you override the emotions that are screaming at you to hide and stay small so that no-one can judge you.

I know for a fact that this is easier said than done though! I remember attending Saturday morning art classes when I was in primary school. I had a bit of talent for art, so my parents figured that I would enjoy being let loose with the pencils and paints and I did.

The art school held an exhibition every year at our local library and this particular year, I was excited about being part of it. I painted the portrait of a girl for my contribution, and all these years later, I can still recall how her dark brown hair framed her face. There was a problem though. I couldn't stop trying to make the picture "perfect." I kept fiddling over and over with the hair to the left of her face, until I ended up with a big chunk of brown paint swerving over her left cheek and obscuring much of her face. The painting still looked oka*yish*, but when I saw it hung in the exhibition my heart sank as I knew the picture had looked far better when I first put down the paint brush a few days prior.

There will be many times where you need to force yourself to stop, put your metaphorical brushes down and let your work go out into the world – and this is where your self-discipline needs to overrule your emotions. The next time that you are tempted to keep fiddling with an already completed project, you need to ask yourself this question: *what am I afraid of?* I can almost guarantee that if you are truly honest with yourself, you will discover that there is something subconscious holding you back from launching, be it fear of judgement, fear of being "caught out" – aka imposter syndrome – fear of looking foolish or some other fear.

I love this acronym about FEAR: *False Evidence Appearing Real.* and the question *"what am I **really** afraid of?"* is the question you need to ask yourself whenever you are resistant to putting your work – or indeed yourself – out there under the guise of it not being perfect.

ACTION STEPS:

- What have you been holding back from sharing with the world? It might be your artworks, your writing, or your new business venture. No matter how large or small, write everything on a list – you might be amazed at how many things you have been procrastinating on launching because they weren't *perfect* enough.
- Work through that list one item at a time, asking yourself the following questions and writing down the answers:
  1. *What am I afraid of?* I'm afraid that people will think that my book sucks.
  2. *What is the worst thing that could happen if I share it?* I might get a bad review.
  3. *What is likely to happen?* People who aren't interested will probably just not read it, and those that do might find that it helps them which is the result I want.
- Now go back through that list and put a circle around the very first item that you will share with the world. If that item is not yet completed, give yourself a date to complete, then follow that with a date to launch it.
- Put a post on your social media to announce that you have something special coming on the date that you wrote down. *Don't be tempted to skip this step!* You are committed now, so do what you need to do to complete your work, then be prepared to put your brush down and proudly reveal your work to the world!

HACK #18
Take Action Every Single Day!

"The path to success is to take massive, determined actions."

~ TONY ROBBINS

How many times have you woken up bright and early on a Monday morning, eager to start your new resolution of exercising for one hour every day? You hit the gym, have a shower and head into the office feeling mighty proud of yourself.

Then comes Tuesday and you have to be at work for a breakfast meeting, so you throw your gym bag into your car with the intent of working out at lunch time. Unfortunately, things get busy and you only get a 20 minute break, so you eat your lunch at your desk and keep working.

Wednesday rolls around and your alarm hasn't gone off so you stagger out of bed too late to get to the gym, but you're not going to make yesterday's mistake! You get your work done in record time so that you can head to the gym on the way home to get that hour of exercise in. You swing out of the car park only to find yourself gridlocked in a massive traffic jam while police cars squeeze past to deal with the accident up ahead. By the time you reach the turn off to your gym, you've already received three phone calls from your partner and your kids asking where you are and what's for dinner. With a sigh, you keep on driving. Once home, you briefly consider making use of the kettlebells laying around in the garage, but you're too knackered after that horrendous commute to bother so grab a glass of wine instead.

Thursday is a repeat of Tuesday with your work day starting with a team breakfast meeting. You throw your gym gear in your car, but don't even bother taking it into the office, as you know that your chances of getting a full hour to workout at lunch time are pretty slim. You toy with the idea of heading to the gym when you begin your drive home but once you reach that turn off, you keep on going. You're tired and fed up. Maybe you can grab an hour to walk after dinner, but deep down, you know that you'll be on the couch with your partner catching the next episode of the Netflix series you've been watching.

Friday rolls around and despite having your gym bag ready, (it's still packed and in your car) you already know that it's not going to see the light of day. Where on earth are you going to find an hour to work out? You plow through your workload and head home for a weekend full of chores, socialising and chilling. You feel pretty blah about not exercising, but you decide to stay positive – after all, you can start again on Monday, and next week will be better ...

Sound familiar? Or is it just me who has repeated this kind of pattern many times – and not just in relation to exercise! Think of those New Year's resolutions you've made over the years – the ones that you stopped talking about by the last week in January when the motivation to completely transform your life had well and truly dissipated ...

The books you never started, let alone finished writing.

The business you never got around to launching.

The holiday savings plan that you never contributed to.

The decluttering that petered out after your first room.

The online course that you never completed.

There is a common denominator with all of these scenarios – *the lack of enough action to bring them to life.* Sure you might have started with great intentions and lots of motivation, however, just like the story of the gym, things got in the way, life happened, and *you let your goal slide.*

Notice however that I didn't say that you were "unable" to meet your goal? It's because most of the time, you not reaching your goal is a decision that YOU have made! Now before you get upset at me, saying *"Cat! I didn't cause the traffic accident that stopped me from going to the gym! I didn't create the extra work that made me miss my lunch break!"* – hear me out!

The simple truth is that life happens, and there will **always** be situations and people to distract you from putting in the time and effort to work on your goals. You can almost guarantee that a family crisis will occur the minute you are about to lock yourself away to do a 3 hour hit on that novel you've been saying forever that you were going to write. I think that children have some weird 6th sense as you can virtually guarantee that yours will get sick on the day of an important meeting that could change your life!

Like I said – life happens, and it will *always* happen – so it is critical to change your thinking about how you approach your goals, and the actions needed to make them happen. Not doing so means that you will **always** be frustrated about how you never achieve anything that you say you want to. I don't know about you, but I don't want to be one of those people who regrets all of the things that they **didn't do** when they get to the end of their life.

Taking *intentional, focused* action on your goals is essential to your success – *right?* Just being busy however will not help you achieve anything other than filling up your time. Your actions need to be laser focused on creating the outcome that you want, HOWEVER – remember that perfectionism we discussed in the last hack? It's time to ditch that in regards to time constraints too …

Going back to our gym analogy: whilst an hour of exercise is a great goal, if you are so black and white about the time rather than the outcome, you will struggle to make progress. If you can use the hour as the *ideal* rather than the rule, you will change your focus. Instead of chasing the number on a clock, you'll find that you are able to slip exercise into your day far more regularly, for instance: you could grab a half hour walk at lunchtime on those days that you couldn't get a complete hour; you could do a fifteen minute HIIT session with a skipping rope on the day of the traffic jam: how about a game of basketball with your kids in your driveway on Friday afternoon when you just want to unwind? All of these are "wins" when you remove the black and white thinking of only a full hour counting as worthwhile. When you think less rigidly about time, you'll find that you are more inclined to take action every day, rather than doing nothing for 6 days when you couldn't create the *perfect* hour long window to go to the gym.

I call these "micro-actions" and doing them daily can be a game-changer.

Regardless of what goal you are chasing, doing micro-actions will not only help nudge you closer to achieving it, but you will be reinforcing your "success muscle" each time that you complete one. The sense of satisfaction you experience at the end of each day you've taken action, will feel so good that you can't wait to do it again! This in turn will make it so much easier for you to create a daily habit – *and it is the daily habits that will help you achieve your goal.*

It's time to stop looking for the "perfect" scenario for you to work towards your goal!

So you don't have a wonderful home office in which to write your novel?

So you don't have a great gym nearby?

So you don't have much money left over each week to save?

It doesn't matter! Start taking micro-actions and stop making excuses!

You can write at the kitchen table and put headphones on if necessary to drown out the family noise!

You can find plenty of free home workouts on YouTube and exercise in your lounge room!

You can save SOMETHING each week, regardless of if it is $5 or $50!

ACTION STEPS:

- Write a list of the goals that you have not yet achieved.
- Be completely honest with yourself and write next to them why you didn't achieve them.
- How many of them were the result of your thinking that you had "no time?" Did you really have no time, or were you waiting for the *perfect* block of time to work in?
- Write 3 micro-actions next to each goal. The idea is that these actions are easily doable, so that when life happens – *which it will* (sorry to break that to you!) – you can quickly regroup and still complete the action. Having flexibility around these actions will give you a far greater chance of success at completing them.

For example: If your dream is to write a book and your daily goal is to write for an hour or complete 1000 words, your 3 micro-actions might be:
   a) Write for 15 minutes before leaving for work.
   b) Write for 15 minutes at lunchtime.
   c) If your word count from these 2 sessions is under 1000, do another brief writing session after dinner to meet that number.

- Print out a monthly planner and pin it up where you will see it often. Every day that you complete your micro-actions, put a cross on that square. You can use

different colours for different goals. The idea is that by the end of the month you have a chain of crosses linked up and stretching across the calendar.
- Create a reward system for yourself. Remember how your teachers used to give you a gold star? Reward yourself for completing 10 days straight or 21 days straight or maybe a full month of daily action. It might be a massage, a pedicure, a movie – whatever you love. Make sure you do it though as you want to reinforce the habit of daily action with positive rewards.

HACK #19
Act Regardless

"Feel the fear and do it anyway!"

~ SUSAN JEFFERS

There are so many great memes that show how growth, opportunity and success come when you are prepared to get out of your comfort zone. These memes were so popular when I was working in the gym for obvious reasons. Those members that *really* wanted to transform their strength and fitness were the ones that got used to being uncomfortable. They rose earlier, trained harder, ate cleaner and partied way less than their less fit counterparts. Working in a gym known for bodybuilding, this dedication to body transformation was even more intense and I witnessed people live with discomfort for months on end in preparation for their 3 minutes on stage. Those that went on to place were awarded pretty cheaply made medals or trophies. We have literally dozens of these in our home, as both my husband and our daughter were title winners, my daughter placing not just in New Zealand, but in Australia and the US as well in the fitness category.

On the surface, the reward of a tin medal or trophy is pitiful compared to the weeks and weeks of dedication and discomfort that the athlete has put themselves through, which begs the question: *why did they do it, over and over, some pushing themselves to compete year after year?*

It's simple really.

Their inner desire to reach their goal was stronger than their desire to remain comfortable.

The desire to step on a stage looking their very best, outweighed their desire to eat what they wanted for 12 weeks or more.

The desire to have the very best physique possible so they could win the title was stronger than their desire to sleep in and not train before and after work.

What do you desire?

Is it strong enough to keep you going at night, or get you up early in the morning to carve out time to work towards making your dream a reality?

Is it powerful enough to help you to stay the course even when people close to you are telling you to "slow down?"

Is it compelling enough to keep you going when it feels like the world is against you?

Those years working in the gym taught me so much about what it means to *really* get out of your comfort zone. They also reminded me of the times in my life where I did achieve things I was proud of, through the process of being uncomfortable ...

The time when I was 11 years old and sat through 3 days of testing and interviews with panels of adults to win a music scholarship to a high school on the other side of the city. This was followed by 5 years of travelling 2 hours either way on buses, lugging instruments along with my school books so I could attend that school. There was nothing comfortable about trying to fit your practice and homework in around 4 hours of commuting a day. While all of the local kids around my home were watching TV and playing, I would either be in a band or choir rehearsal or sitting on a bus every evening.

Those years built my "discomfort muscle" however, and once I finished school, I jumped on a bus at age 17 to travel for 3 days across the Australian Nullabour, to repeat virtually the same process of 3 days of auditions, interviews and tests to vie for a place at the Sydney Conservatorium of Music. I won a place and the next four years saw me doing the same thing I had been doing since age 11 – spending 4 hours a day lugging instruments as I commuted back and forth, and trying to juggle my studies, my part time music teaching job, my weekend garage band rehearsals, my gigs, and my instrumental practice.

It was uncomfortable, but I did it, and looking back, I sometimes wonder how I managed to sustain such a huge commitment for 9 years of my life. It all comes down to one thing though – my desire to perform on stage as a musician was stronger than my desire for comfort.

There are so many other examples of where my desire for the goal was stronger than my desire to remain comfortable and I'm sure that if you sat and thought about it, you would have plenty of examples too. For an introvert, putting myself out there whenever I wrote a book, recorded a CD or stepped on stage was definitely going out of my comfort zone. Competing in a women's Triathlon just before I turned 40, a year after a complicated hysterectomy was way out of my comfort zone! In each case though, the desire to succeed pushed me through the early morning training sessions, made me face the computer and keep writing, kept me practicing my instrument and stopped me from shying away from the stage.

Maybe you are thinking "well I haven't written a book or done anything like that," but I can guarantee that there are times in your life where you pushed yourself out of your comfort zone too. What about those years when you were tired to the bone, caring for a baby or a grizzly toddler and trying to stay on top of your job? It would have been so much more comfortable to dump your children at your parents, take time off work and go home to sleep, but you didn't do it did you? You got yourself up and you fed and changed them. You washed their clothes, you showed them love and patience and kept a professional demeanour in your workplace even when you were exhausted

How about that time when you were working long hours, then when you arrived home shattered, you cooked dinner, supervised homework, fed pets and tidied up? Every part of your body was screaming to collapse and put your feet up, but you didn't. You were uncomfortable, but you stayed that way until your family were fed and cared for and the kids finally bathed and tucked up in bed.

You have been outside of your comfort zone before, and you have within you the capability to do so again – but here's the clincher: *You will only be able to do it if your purpose is stronger than your comfort.*

So is it?

Is the work that you are wanting to do in your next season a strong enough motivator for you?

Are you so passionate about it that you will do what needs to be done – no matter how uncomfortable you might feel at times?

We are at the section in the book where the rubber now meets the road. You don't usually get to your 40s, 50s and beyond and choose to add something to your life that feels like a chore. Chances are you've had years, if not decades of "working for the man." You know that creating something purposeful and significant is going to take effort – so you need to decide now if your passion for your mission is strong enough to keep you going when you find yourself uncomfortable – because I can assure you, those times will come!

ACTION STEPS:

- Pull up your notes from all of the action steps thus far and re-read them. Take 30 minutes to really think and pray about them. How do you feel when you are reading about what you want to do in your next season? Excited? Invigorated? Obligated? Doubtful?
- If you feel like there is a weight on you, now is the time to consider if this really is the right direction for you. Sure there will be tough times – there is with any venture – but you should be feeling excited and optimistic at the start of your new season, not dreading it.
- Feeling unsure? This is the time to seek out one or two of your dream team members. Ask for their thoughts on what it is that you are considering. Ask them where they can see potential pitfalls and brainstorm those scenarios.
- Feeling excited about what is to come? Close your eyes and lean into that feeling while creating a visual image that is reinforced with all of your senses. This feeling is the one that will help you when it is time to get uncomfortable. *Remember it!*

SECTION 7

LEGACY

"If you would not be forgotten as soon as you are dead, either write something worth reading or do something worth writing."

~ BENJAMIN FRANKLIN

HACK #20
Design your Legacy

> "The great use of life is to spend it for something that will outlast it."
>
> ~ WILLIAM JAMES

My husband celebrated his 60th birthday in January 2020, and he had the best night with an amazing cake and many wonderful friends present to celebrate with him. There was one word that kept coming to mind that night however, and I wrote the following post about it a few days later:

As you can imagine, turning 60 causes you to stop and ask yourself a lot of questions, and my husband has certainly been doing so:

Am I living the life that I wanted to live?

Do I have the career, family and home that I wanted?

Have I created the LEGACY I intended to create?

As you might already know, due to the 2019 that I experienced, I have been asking myself these questions too, the main one being about what legacy I want to leave.

Regardless of whether my husband feels that he has achieved all that he intended or not, there was one profound legacy of his that was revealed at his party. Four different friends of his that I asked to speak, all ended up saying the same thing: "He loves his family so much."

Needless to say, the impact of that legacy of love for our children and for me is powerful.

As I've mentioned before, there is an internal shift that takes place at midlife. Many find that the driving force behind their decisions is no longer ambition and striving to be "successful". Instead, it is a desire to create something that will outlive them – a quest to be "significant".

It might be business related, it might be charitable or it might simply be to build a legacy of love that undergirds your family. Your legacy is the imprint you leave on the hearts and minds of the people in your life, and if ever there were a time to consider how that imprint will look – it is at midlife.

I was asked just this morning what my memorial plans were by one of the women in my Midlife Entrepreneur Success Community for Women group. I had to confess that I've not thought about the kind of funeral I want at all. I suppose that I should, given that I have lost good friends over the past few years at younger ages than I am now, however whilst I haven't written down what songs I want at my funeral, I *have* put a lot of thought already into the legacy I want to leave:

I want my Rocking Midlife® mission of inspiring women to live their second season with purpose and passion to continue.

I want to leave my family and the world a collection of books that I have written.

I want to leave my children and grandchildren a legacy of love and courage to fulfil the dreams and visions that they have for their lives.

I want to leave a financial legacy that blesses not only my family but enables local charitable organisations that I support to keep their good work going.

It's not morbid to be thinking of what your legacy will be, in fact it is quite the opposite. Once you have that clear picture in mind, you can reverse engineer it and work out what you need to be doing *right now* to create that legacy.

Think of the people in your life. Think of the things that you are passionate about – art, music, causes such as children with cancer, or helping the elderly with dementia.

Your legacy doesn't have to be tied to finances, nor does it need to be tangible like leaving amazing paintings or artworks. Your legacy could be the story of your devotion and care that is remembered at the hospital you volunteered at for so many years. Your legacy might be that you are remembered by the hundreds of students who knew you as a teacher who genuinely cared.

Not taking the time to think about your legacy means that you risk drifting through your midlife years and beyond, never feeling fully "on task" or content. There's nothing more frustrating than those times when you know that you want to make a difference in the world – but you just don't know what that is. Instead of reading self-help book after self-help book in order to "find yourself," – why not simply ask yourself *"what legacy do I want to leave?"*

As you can tell, I'm a great believer in simple, practical actions, and I can assure you that answering this question will be the very thing to give purpose and direction to your life. You won't have to look wide eyed like a rabbit caught in the headlights any longer when someone asks you what your life-purpose is. You'll already know because it is part and parcel of the legacy you want to leave in the world.

Imagine not having to go live like a monk in some far-flung place in order to discover your purpose in life!

Imagine not having to search high and low for some guru to tell you what you *should* be doing with your life?

The answer to your life purpose is deep inside you.

You just need to ask this question: *what's my legacy?*

ACTION STEPS:

- Make a date with yourself. Put it in your diary and KEEP IT!
- Have your date in a location that is peaceful, and remove all distractions – that includes your phone as well as people!
- Grab a pen and paper and write your eulogy. *Yes – your eulogy!* Write down all the things that you would hope to hear at your funeral.
- What stands out? Are there things in that eulogy you are yet to complete?
- Pray and meditate over these things. Roll them over in your mind and see them as done. How does that make you *feel?*
- Write a list of the things that you want to be part of your legacy. These can be a mix of physical, financial and emotional things.
- Circle the ones that you need to start working on now. For instance, you may have written that you want to create a financial legacy for your grandchildren, so your action now would be to open an account in their name and start saving a small amount each week for them.

HACK #21

Own your Own Spotlight!

"Step into your power. Fearlessly and graciously, walk your path."

~ ANGELA GWINNER

Have you ever stood in the wings of a stage, waiting for your moment to go on with a stomach full of butterflies and knees quivering like jelly?

As someone who has spent so many hours of my life on stages in front of various crowds across the world, I can tell you that stage fright is a very real thing and I experienced it horribly when I was in high school and at university. The mid year and end of year practical performance exams I had to endure were excruciating.

I recall standing in front of examiners, messing up scales that I could normally play without a second thought.

I recall walking out of exams in tears after making mistakes that were so basic.

I recall singing a duet in latin with a friend in front of my church and my leg shaking so badly that I was certain that everyone was laughing at me.

I recall feeling physically ill so many times when I was asked to play or sing a line on my own in front of the huge choir or concert band.

For so many years I faced fear, lack of confidence and self doubt, and every single performance was a battle between my desire to perform and my desire to run and give the whole game up as a bad joke.

I haven't really leaned into the emotions of those experiences until now, so many decades later. I basically shoved them to the back of my mind as being too painful to dwell on. Back then, I considered myself an extremely plain, average girl – and there were mean girls who certainly reinforced my thinking. Despite this however, I desperately wanted to do and become more, and with the hindsight that comes with age and experience, I can see now that I was actually incredibly hard working and focussed.

During those 9 years of school and university, I juggled commuting, practicing, homework, assignments, having to learn other instruments, rehearsals, part time work, church and youth group commitments, family life, friends and boyfriends. I could so easily have given it all up and gone to the local school down the road, followed by the local university like all of my school friends ... yet it never entered my mind.

I had a dream, and I worked towards it – even though it was hard and scary and meant putting myself in uncomfortable position after uncomfortable position – and I've continued to push myself to this day.

Why?

Because even in my youth, I instinctively knew that I only had one shot of creating the life I wanted – and that is still the case today.

There are no do-overs.

If you let fear and trembling prevent you from walking out onto the stage of your life – be it as a writer, an entrepreneur, an artist – *whatever* – you risk never having that opportunity again.

If your second season – your midlife years and beyond – are to truly ROCK – you need to step into your spotlight and own your stage *now*. Time is no longer on your side. You don't know what tomorrow will bring, so if ever you were going to step up and live your life to the fullest – it is now.

There is one presentation that I often give when speaking to groups of women, titled *Are you the Leading Lady of your Life?* In it, I share so much of what I have written in this book. I encourage my audience with the names and faces of famous women who stepped into their greatness in their midlife seasons, and I remind them that they need to truly own the leading lady role in their own lives instead of deferring that role to other people – something we women often do so easily.

As we near the end of this book, I want to grab you by the shoulders, (in love of course!) and remind you that you are an amazing, unique woman whose time is NOW.

You have raised your family.

You have loved and lost – possibly a few times over – and you are still here.

You are resilient and brave – after all, you are still standing …

And your personal spotlight is waiting for you to step into it.

When my closest girlfriend died on the morning of my son's wedding in 2019, and my highest and lowest moments of the year clashed in a day of emotion – I felt the reality of the ticking of time as never before.

Here was my first born child, the man who had been my baby boy, speaking his vows to his lovely wife. (As I write this book, they are now the proud – and exhausted – parents of their own baby boy.) At the same time, my friend who had been like a sister to me for 20 years was gone. Her life was finished at 57.

If ever there was a picture of the circle of life, this was it.

Our days are not promised.

Our life on earth is not forever.

We only have this moment – so how will you act?

What will you do?

Who will you become?

Will you be brave enough to stand against the naysayers, the mean girls, the doubters, your own fear and create that legacy, that life of purpose and significance that you say you want to create?

The time is now.

Your spotlight is ready.

The people who need your wisdom are waiting.

Your legacy is waiting to be built.

ACTION STEPS:

- What are you fearful of? Write it down.
- Why are you fearful? Take the time to read through the "what" and think about if your fears are logical or perceived.
- What are you wanting to do or become in your next season? Write it down and go back to your visualisation exercise, picturing you being this person, feeling how powerful and confident you are.
- Do a definitive action to mark that today really is the *"first day of the rest of your life."* Put a big red circle on your calendar and write a power statement that you stick on your bathroom mirror to see every morning. An example might be *"I am a transformative, fully booked international speaker and coach who is creating a legacy of midlife women who believe that their second season can be powerful, and creating a ripple effect of positive impact on their families and communities."*
- Read your power statement Every. Single. Day. Choose to be that person now. Not tomorrow, not when you've researched, read and studied some more. Choose to be that person today. That person who understands that time is fleeting and that now is the time to truly live your life ON purpose and impact your world for the better.
- Step into your spotlight beautiful.

A FINAL WORD FROM CAT

You've got this.

You are an amazing woman and you have incredible God given gifts and talents that are as unique as you are. Your world needs you to shine and share those gifts so that your family, your friends, your community can be positively impacted.

My hope is that these 21 Hacks give you hope, as well as prompt you to take real, intentional action to bring your dreams and goals for your midlife years to life. So many people skim read books like this, however my hope is that you will truly dig deep and create the second season that you truly aspire to …

One that is significant.

One that is liberating as you openly share your real self with the world.

One that is impactful as you make a difference to those around you and purposely work towards creating a legacy that will last long after you are gone.

One that is empowering and fulfilling for you and inspiring and motivating for those who walk behind in your footsteps.

I read somewhere that midlife is not for pussies – and you, my friend, are no pussy.

Live with purpose, with passion, and most of all – *here's to Rocking Midlife!*

Cat x

ABOUT CAT COLUCCIO

Cat Coluccio is an Author, a Reinvention Coach, the host of the **Rocking Midlife® Podcast** and **Community** – *and a champion of midlife women.*

A qualified Educator, Personal Trainer and Life Coach, Cat is passionate about seeing women empowered to stop procrastinating, identify their values and goals, take intentional action and build purposeful lives and businesses, creating a legacy for their families and communities.

At home speaking on both live or virtual stages, Cat has been a featured guest on numerous international podcasts and summits, as well as in national print publications, television and radio shows.

A transplanted Australian, Cat resides in New Zealand with her husband, children and grandson, along with far too many cats, chooks and sheep. She's partial to a glass of prosecco and a laugh with friends, good chocolate, great books, and lives by her personal philosophy: *"It's never too late to have a new beginning in life."*

WANT MORE CAT?

Check out Cat's other 21 Hacks books!

21 Hacks to ROCK your Life!
*Stop Procrastinating, Do that Thing
and Live your Life ON-Purpose!*

21 Hacks to ROCK your Life – the TEEN Edition!
*Stop Stuffing Around, Get Focused
and Create a Life that ROCKS!!*

Find these titles and more by following
Cat's author page HERE: https://amzn.to/3A2XoKu

Want more FREE resources to help you ROCK your life?

Check out Cat's website HERE: www.catcoluccio.com

Let's get Social!

F: @catoluccio
IG: @catcoluccio
Pin: @catcoluccio
YT: @catcoluccio

Want some cool clothing, gifts and motivating printables?

Check out Cat's 2 ETSY shops HERE:

Rocking Midlife®:
https://www.etsy.com/nz/shop/rockingmidlife

Rock your Side-Hustle:
https://www.etsy.com/nz/shop/RockyourSideHustle

Join Cat daily in her FREE community for women – Rocking Midlife® – for support, encouragement and a whole lot of laughs!

www.facebook.com/groups/RockingMidlife/

ACKNOWLEDGEMENTS

I continue to be grateful to the man who still has my back after 33 years together. Leli, you are an incredible husband, father and nonno and I am especially grateful that you broke the traditional patriarchal framework you were raised in to become a God fearing, vacuum wielding, BBQ master who keeps our house clean and us all fed when I am lost in the black hole of editing!

As well, I am so blessed to have had the challenge of trying to write this set of 21 Hacks while fielding visits from my gorgeous grandson. I might have slipped up on living up to my productivity hacks from the original 21 Hacks book, but I wouldn't change it for the world!

To the team at Indie-Experts headed up by the amazing Dixie and Ann – I am grateful again for your support, kindness and generosity in helping me launch yet another book into the world. I am so excited for our combined mission to help other authors get their stories out there and look forward to what's to come!

This book is dedicated to the women in my Rocking Midlife® FB group – many of whom have shared the ups and downs of their midlife journey with me for years now. I am indebted to those who kindly proofread the *21 Hacks to ROCK your Midlife* manuscript, and love that these ladies represent the truly international feel of our group: Tejwant Chahal in India, Betina Naidoo in South Africa, Sue Baker in the US and Yanina Purcell in New Zealand. Thank you SO much for your time and suggestions!

A massive thank you to US based Catherine Grace O'Connell for writing the foreword to this book. Catherine is as beautiful inside as she is outside and shares a similar mission of encouraging women to break through ageism and embrace their midlife years through her group Forever Fierce – Midlife Matters.

To my children, daughter in law, mum and dad and greater family – you guys are my world and I love you all dearly, regardless of what country wins the rugby or cricket!

Finally, I want to give a shout out to my beautiful sister in law Angela who faced her own mortality over the past year as she battled cancer. You are an incredible mother, wife and woman and I know that the legacy of love that you have built with your family is one that will impact them for generations to come. Love you sis x

Cat x

Auckland, June 2021

www.ingramcontent.com/pod-product-compliance
Lightning Source LLC
Chambersburg PA
CBHW050313010526
44107CB00055B/2224